NUTSHELLS

FAMILY LAW
IN A NUTSHELL

THIRD EDITION

by

Tony Wragg
Senior Lecturer in Law,
University of Derby

London ● Sweet & Maxwell ● 1995

Published in 1995 by
Sweet & Maxwell Limited of
100 Avenue Road, Swiss Cottage, London NW3 3PF
Computerset by
Wyvern Typesetting Limited, Bristol
Printed in England by Clays Ltd., St Ives plc

Reprinted 1996

A CIP catalogue record
for this book is available
from the British Library

ISBN 0–421–533102

CONTENTS

TABLE OF ABBREVIATIONS

CA	Children Act 1989
CSA	Child Support Act 1991
C.C.A.	County Courts Act 1984
D.P.M.C.A.	Domestic Proceedings and Magistrates Court Act 1978
D.V.A.	Domestic Violence and Matrimonial Proceedings Act 1976
F.L.R.A.	Family Law Reform Act 1987
H.F.E.A.	Human Fertilisation and Embryology Act 1990
M.C.A.	Matrimonial Causes Act 1973
M.F.P.A.	Matrimonial and Family Proceedings Act 1984
S.C.A.	Supreme Courts Act 1981

NOTE: The abbreviation "C.A." is also used, *in a case reference*, to mean Court of Appeal.

THE LAW STATED IS AS AT 31ST AUGUST 1994.

1. DECREES RELATING TO MARRIAGE

DIVORCE

The Ground for Divorce and the Five Facts

There is only one ground for divorce: the petitioner must establish
that the marriage has irretrievably broken down (M.C.A., s. 1(1)).
However, the court cannot grant a divorce unless the petitioner
also proves one of five facts, as referred to in the M.C.A., s. 1(2).

The five facts are:

(a) that the respondent has committed adultery and the petitioner finds it intolerable to live with him

(b) that the respondent has behaved in such a way that the
petitioner cannot reasonably be expected to live with him

(c) that the respondent has deserted the petitioner for a period
of at least two years immediately preceding the presentation
of the petition

(d) that the parties have lived apart for a continuous period
of at least two years immediately preceding the presentation
of the petition and the respondent consents to a decree
being granted

(e) that the parties have lived apart for a period of at least
five years immediately preceding the presentation of the
petition.

It must be emphasised that even if the court reaches the conclusion
that the marriage has irretrievably broken down, a decree cannot
be granted unless the petitioner also proves one of the five facts
(see, for example, *Chilton* v. *Chilton* (C.A. 1990)). However, proof
of one of the five facts does not conclusively establish irretrievable
breakdown: the court can still refuse a decree if it is satisfied that
the marriage has not irretrievably broken down (M.C.A., s. 1(4)).
However, the petitioner need not prove that the fact established
caused the irretrievable breakdown.

It should be noted that by section 3 of the M.C.A. no petition
for divorce can be filed until the parties have been married for
one year. This is an absolute bar to divorce; the court has no

discretion to waive this requirement. Nevertheless, a divorce petition filed at any time after this period may include references to
matters or events arising or occurring during this period.

Consideration will now be given to each of the five facts in turn.

Section 1(2)(a)

This fact has two limbs. It is established that the second limb—
the petitioner's finding it intolerable to live with the respondent—
does not have to be caused by the first limb—the respondent's
adultery (*Cleary* v. *Cleary* (C.A. 1974)). This decision was reluct-
antly given and provoked criticism not least because of the odd
results it could produce.

Adultery has been defined as "willing sexual intercourse between
a married person and one of the opposite sex" (*S* v. *S* (H.C.
1962)).

"Sexual intercourse" means penetration of the female by the
male, however briefly *Dennis* v. (*Dennis* (C.A. 1955)).

"Willing" connotes, first, that the person against whom the
allegation is made should have consented to the intercourse. Thus,
a woman who is raped does not thereby commit adultery.

Secondly, "willing" connotes that person has the necessary
capacity to form the intent to commit adultery.

S. v. S.

> The husband had committed adultery with a lady insane within the
> definition of the McNaghten rules. She was held not to have committed
> adultery and dismissed from the suit.

However, if the alleged adulterer lacked capacity as a result of
voluntarily consuming excess alcohol, adultery can still be found
against him. The court will examine the surrounding circumstances, including the motive for drinking, in determining whether
or not that party was guilty of adultery (*Goshawk* v. *Goshawk* (H.C.
1965)).

Dealing now with the issue of intolerability, the wording of the
M.C.A. itself suggests that the test that the court should apply
is a subjective one, *i.e.* whether *this* petitioner finds it intolerable
to live with the respondent (and not whether a reasonable petitioner finds it intolerable to live with the respondent). The subject-

ive test has been confirmed as being the correct one in *Goodrich* v. *Goodrich* (H.C. 1971).

Section 2(1) of the M.C.A. provides that there can be no decree if the parties have lived with each other for more than six months after the *discovery* of the alleged adultery.

Section 1(2)(b)

One of the best formulations of the principles to be applied in deciding whether or not this fact is proved is to be found in *Livingstone-Stallard* v. *Livingstone-Stallard* (H.C. 1974). According to Dunn J., the question that must be answered in the affirmative is:

> "Would any right thinking person come to the conclusion that this husband has behaved in such a way that this wife cannot reasonably be expected to live with him, taking into account the whole of the circumstances and the characters and personalities of the parties?"

The principle applies equally where it is the husband who is the petitioner.

There is an objective element in this test but it should also be noted that the test takes into account the characters and personalities of the actual parties concerned. This will mean, for example, that if a particular petitioner is a weak or timid character then it is likely that the court would not expect him to endure a level of conduct that it may expect a stronger or more forceful petitioner to withstand. Similarly, the petitioner's own conduct may be relevant as where, for example, the respondent's behaviour has been provoked.

As each case stands or falls on its own facts, it is of little use to cite numerous authorities detailing the type of behaviour that has been held to be sufficient under this fact. Such matters as violence, obsessive gambling, excessive drinking and conducting amorous, even if not adulterous, relationships with others, will usually amount to behaviour that the petitioner cannot reasonably be expected to put up with and this is perhaps not surprising.

However, conduct that on the face of it is more trivial than that already mentioned, can also amount to such behaviour if, for example, the petitioner is able to show that the conduct complained of has occurred consistently over an appreciable period of time. In this category would be such matters as threats, addressing the petitioner with abuse and/or obscene language, criticism or humiliation.

The courts have identified two types of behaviour, positive and negative or, to put it another way, acts and omissions.

It is not necessary for the respondent to have intended to harm or distress the petitioner with his behaviour or even to have intended to behave in a particular way at all.

Thurlow v. Thurlow

The wife was an epileptic and suffering from a neurological disorder. As a result, over a period of a few years, her physical condition deteriorated until she became bedridden, doubly incontinent and needed assistance in feeding. During her illness, she had also caused worry by setting fire to articles of clothing and furniture, wandering in the streets at night and throwing small household items at her mother-in-law. The husband, who had made valiant efforts to cope with looking after her, was granted a decree.

Carter-Fea v. Carter-Fea (1987)

He was unable to manage his affairs. Wife found it impossible to live in "a world of fantasy, with unpaid bills, bailiffs at the door and second mortgages".

But the behaviour must be more than "just a state of affairs".

Pheasant v. Pheasant (1972)

Husband complained that wife did not give him the "spontaneous, demonstrative affection which he craved". The petition failed: they had simply become incompatible.

Petitions based on this ground remain a striking example of the failure of the legislation to eliminate bitterness and humiliation from divorce. For example

Livingstone-Stallard v. Livingstone-Stallard

The husband made a long list of trivial complaints, including disputes about washing underwear and "drinking with tradespeople".

Mason v. Mason (1980)

How often should couples have sex?

Richards v. Richards (1974)

Amongst the wife's catalogue of complaints was the fact that he forgot her birthday and didn't buy her flowers at the birth of the child.

With regard to the provisions for living together, section 2 does not contain an absolute prohibition relating to petitions under the M.C.A., s.1(2)(b). If the parties have lived with each other after the date of the last incident of behaviour alleged in the petition, then this fact is to be disregarded if they have not done so for more than six months. By implication, therefore, the court can take into account the fact that the parties have lived with each other for a period exceeding six months after the date of the last incident of behaviour alleged, when assessing whether or not the fact for divorce has been established. Thus, section 2 creates a discretionary bar to divorce for petitions under the M.C.A., s.1(2)(b).

Section 1(2)(c)

Approximately one per cent. of divorce petitions presented rely on desertion. The concept will therefore be only briefly discussed.

There are four conditions that must be fulfilled before a spouse will be found to be in desertion:

(a) the parties must be physically living apart
(b) the deserting spouse must have the requisite intention
(c) the separation must not have taken place as a result of an agreement between the parties
(d) the deserting spouse must not have had good cause for leaving.

(a) *The physical separation.* This concept will be discussed in connection with section 1(2)(d) of the M.C.A.

(b) *The intention.* The petitioner must establish that the respondent intended to live apart permanently. Clearly, this means that the respondent must also have had the capacity to form that intention.

(c) *Lack of agreement.* Such an agreement can be expressed, as where the parties enter into a formal written separation agreement, or implied from their conduct.

(d) *Lack of good cause.* Most cases of the respondent's having good cause for leaving arise from the petitioner's conduct, but it is not the only reason.

In theory, it would seem impossible for the good cause for leaving to arise, for example, as a result of the alleged deserter being medically advised to live apart from his spouse permanently.

Further, desertion can be terminated by one of the conditions ceasing to exist. This general statement is subject to many qualifications, that will not be discussed.

For a decree to be granted on the basis of desertion, it must have lasted for a continuous period of two years immediately preceding the presentation of the divorce petition. This means that the four conditions that must exist before desertion can start to run, must continue in existence for at least two years, without a break, right up to the date of issue of the divorce petition. However, it should be noted that section 2(5) provides the "continuous nature of the separation is not to be affected by the parties having lived with each other for a period of less than six months, though no account shall be taken of that period in calculating the length of separation". For example, H. left in January 1993, returned in January 1994 for three months, then left again. Petition could not be presented until April 1995 (two years desertion plus three months of cohabitation).

Section 1(2)(d)

The fact has two limbs: a period of living apart and the respondent's consent.

It is usually quite easy to determine that the parties are "living apart" in the physical sense. Most often, one spouse will move out of the home and go and live elsewhere. However, by section 2(6) of the M.C.A., the parties are to be treated as living apart "unless they are living with each other in the same household." This provision, therefore, makes it possible for the parties to obtain a divorce under section 1(2)(d) even though they are living under the same roof, if they are living in such a way that they can be said to have established separate households. Generally this means that any sign of a communal or joint life must be absent.

Le Brocq v. Le Brocq (1964)

Wife excluded husband from her bedroom by means of a bolt on the door: they spoke to each other only when necessary. But she cooked his meals and he paid her weekly housekeeping. Per Harman L.J.: "There was a separation of bedrooms, separation of hearts—but one household was carried on."

Mouncer v. Mouncer (H.C. 1972)

The parties had separate bedrooms and the wife did not do the husband's washing. Nevertheless, the wife cooked for the family and the parties took their meals together. Both were responsible for the cleaning. The husband had refused to move out because he wanted to see and care for the children.

Held: the parties were still living with each other in the same household.

The lack of a communal life is not always the key however.

Fuller v. *Fuller* (C.A. 1973)

Four years after the wife left the husband to go and live with another man, the husband became ill and was not well enough to live by himself. He moved in with the wife and her boyfriend, as a lodger, so that the wife could nurse him. The parties had separate bedrooms—indeed the wife slept with her boyfriend—but the wife cooked and washed for the husband.

Held: the parties were not living with each other in the same household because this phrase meant living with each other as husband and wife.

The concept of living apart does not only entail the physical separation of the parties. As was stated in *Santos* v. *Santos* (C.A. 1972):

"it is necessary to prove something more than that the husband and the wife are physically separated . . . the relevant state of affairs does not exist whilst both parties recognise the marriage as still subsisting."

However, it is sufficient that one of the parties recognised that the marriage was at an end (even if this is the petitioner) and it is not necessary for that party to communicate the recognition to the other.

Therefore, if the parties separate because, for example, one of them is committed to prison or goes to work abroad and, at the time, both feel that the marriage is still alive, section 1(2)(d) cannot be used for divorce or at least, not until one of the parties has changed his mind about the state of the marriage and has then waited two years.

For the court to find that the marriage has irretrievably broken down on the basis that the parties have lived apart, they must have done so for at least two years immediately preceding the presentation of the petition. Subject to the M.C.A., s. 2, this means that both elements of the concept of living apart must exist for two years, without a break, right up to the date of issuing the divorce petition.

Under the M.C.A., s. 1(2)(d), the respondent's consent to the decree is necessary. He must therefore have the mental capacity to give that consent. This involves the respondent not only knowing what he is doing in giving consent but also understanding the consequences (*Mason* v. *Mason* (H.C. 1972)).

Section 1(2)(e)

There are three significant differences between this subsection and the previous one: the length of time the parties have to have been separated, the lack of the requirement of the respondent's consent, and the defence created by the M.C.A., s. 5 (see below).

Otherwise, the two facts are identical in law. The definition of "living apart," applies to section 1(2)(e) also; while the facts of *Santos* v. *Santos* involved a petition under section 1(2)(d), it was made quite clear that the necessity for at least one of the parties to have felt that the marriage was dead before they could be said to be "living apart" was equally applicable to petitions under section 1(2)(e).

Although facts (d) and (e) are so similar in law it is to be remembered that their use in practice is very different. Parties will use section 1(2)(d) when they agree that there should be a divorce, and the subsequent proceedings are often completely amicable. Petitions under section 1(2)(e) are often filed when one party is totally against the idea: as a result, the proceedings are often acrimonious.

Section 5 of the M.C.A. creates a defence to divorce available only to respondents to petitions based on five years separation. If the court finds that the petitioner can establish another fact for divorce, as well as that under the M.C.A., s. 1(2)(e), then the defence under section 5 is not available. The respondent must establish that the dissolution of the marriage would result in "grave financial or other hardship to him and that it would in all the circumstances be wrong to dissolve the marriage." This defence is rarely pleaded and rarely successful.

It must be emphasised that the hardship must result from the dissolution of the marriage and not the separation of the parties. This probably explains why there are few reported cases on this topic: in practice, any hardship suffered by the respondent has usually arisen as a result of the separation long before.

Grenfell v. *Grenfell* (C.A. 1978)

Wife objected to divorce as a Greek Orthodox whose conscience would be affronted. Not sufficiently "grave".

Reiterbund v. *Reiterbund* (C.A. 1975)

Wife aged 52, husband aged 54. She would lose widow's pension if he were to die within eight years. Court thought there was little risk of him dying in that time, and in any event, state benefits would have compensated her. The decree was granted.

Julian v. *Julian* (1972)

He was 61, she was 58, both in poor health. He paid her maintenance but that would die with him. She would lose police widow's pension if divorce were allowed. A rare example of the court refusing to grant a decree.

Any respondent is entitled to defend a divorce petition on the basis that the fact for divorce alleged does not exist, but these cases are rare.

It should be noted that if the respondent is successful in defending the divorce petition, in whatever way, the marriage will not be terminated. This situation must be distinguished from a respondent who succeeds, not only in defending a divorce petition, but also in cross petitioning himself: that is in successfully establishing a fact for divorce against the petitioner. The result will then be that the marriage is terminated but that it is the respondent who has obtained the decree.

Delays

A delay in the divorce process can occur for many reasons: inertia or a lack of co-operation on the part of one of the parties or the petitioner's solicitor having too great a work load. However, delay can also occur as a result of the operation of sections 10 and 41 of the M.C.A., both of which are designed to ensure that the interests of persons other than the petitioner enjoy a certain measure of protection in the divorce process. A divorce is granted in two stages: decree nisi and then, usually just a few weeks later, decree absolute. Both sections 10 and 41 of the M.C.A. can operate to delay the grant of a decree absolute of divorce, even though the nisi has been granted on proof of irretrievable breakdown.

Section 10 of the M.C.A. enables the respondent to a divorce based upon either two or five years' separation to apply to the court, after the grant of a decree nisi but before the grant of a decree absolute, for his financial position to be considered. Basically, no grant of a decree absolute is then possible until the court is satisfied with the arrangements made for the respondent. This can result in a long delay.

Section 41 of the M.C.A., as amended by the CA, is designed to protect children. Note, however, that only certain children receive the protection afforded by the section. First, a child must be a "child of the family," a concept that will be considered in more detail later (see Chapter 6). Secondly, he must be under 16 (unless the court directs that an older child should receive the protection of the section).

In all cases, the court must consider whether or not there are relevant children. If there are, the court must then consider whether it is likely to have to exercise any of its powers under the CA in respect of them (the court's powers under the CA will be discussed more fully in Chapters 7 and 8, but, for example, include the power to make orders determining with whom the child shall live and/or have contact, and the power to order a local authority to investigate the child's circumstances).

If both of these questions are answered in the affirmative, then, subject to two further conditions, the court can direct that a decree absolute of divorce should not be granted without further order of the court. To summarise, the two further conditions are:

(a) that the court is not in a position to exercise its CA powers without further consideration of the case and

(b) that there are exceptional circumstances that make it desirable in the interests of the child to make a direction.

There is scope in this section for a considerable amount of variation in the type of situations that will lead to a direction: what one judge considers "exceptional" another will not. But whenever the court does make a direction, the grant of the decree absolute will have to wait.

JUDICIAL SEPARATION

Most people whose marriages have broken down will proceed to divorce. There are some, however, who do not wish to terminate the marriage, for example, because of religious objections. Nevertheless, such people often require some recognition of the breakdown and a decree of judicial separation can fill this need. It does not terminate the marriage: it simply relieves the petitioner of the duty to cohabit with the respondent (M.C.A., s. 18(1)).

Others will institute proceedings for judicial separation not because they want a decree for its own sake but because they wish to obtain one of the very wide financial orders that the court can make once a decree of judicial separation has been made. Such wide orders, made under the M.C.A., s. 24, are only possible after a decree of nullity or divorce or judicial separation. It may be impossible for some people to obtain either of the first two mentioned decrees or they simply may not yet be ready to apply for a decree that terminates the marriage.

The Grounds for Judicial Separation

By section 17(1) of the M.C.A., there are five grounds and they correspond exactly with the five facts for divorce created by the M.C.A., s. 1(2). There is no need to establish that the marriage has irretrievably broken down.

Bars, Defences and Delays to Judicial Separation

Bars

There is no time bar on the presentation of a petition for judicial separation. Theoretically, parties can marry on one day and then one of them can present a petition for judicial separation the next. Given that the grounds for judicial separation are the same as the facts for divorce, if a person is able to petition for the former but not the latter, it will usually be because of the absence of a time bar on the former.

However, the provisions of the M.C.A., s. 2 (relating to the parties having lived with each other) apply equally to proceedings for judicial separation.

Defences

A respondent to a petition for judicial separation may defend upon the basis that the ground does not exist, but the defence of grave financial or other hardship is not available.

Delays

The provisions of the M.C.A., s. 41 (relating to protection for the children) apply to proceedings for judicial separation. Thus, even where one of the grounds are proved, a court can delay a decree of judicial separation by directing that it should not be granted without further order (as a decree of judicial separation is granted in one stage, not two, it is the decree itself that is delayed). As with divorce, in practice, the decree will be withheld until such time as the court is able to exercise its CA powers or until such time as it can be persuaded that the circumstances are no longer exceptional.

Section 10 of the M.C.A. does not apply to judicial separation proceedings.

NULLITY

The third type of decree that the divorce court can grant is one of nullity. As can be gathered from the word, such a decree declares the marriage to be null and void which is different from terminating it. The distinction is subtle, but important for those whose personal beliefs do not include divorce. Nevertheless, a decree of nullity ends the marriage in the same way as divorce, in the sense that the parties to it are free to marry thereafter. Less than half a per cent. of petitions presented are petitions for nullity. Therefore the subject will be only briefly discussed.

Void and Voidable Marriages

A void marriage is one that was never a marriage at all, right from the day of its apparent celebration. As a result, at law, it is not necessary for the parties to a void marriage to obtain a decree of nullity before they are entitled to act as single people. (They usually do however: the court's powers to grant financial relief under the M.C.A., ss. 23 & 24 (see Chapter 2) are available only where a decree has been granted.)

A voidable marriage, on the other hand, is a valid marriage until annulled by decree. As a result, the parties to such a marriage must obtain a decree before they are entitled to behave as single people.

The Grounds for Nullity

Section 11 of the M.C.A. details the four grounds that are available for declaring a marriage void. They are:

(a) that it is not a valid marriage under the Marriage Acts 1949–86

(b) that at the time of the marriage either party was already lawfully married

(c) that the parties are not respectively male and female
(d) in the case of a polygamous marriage entered into outside England and Wales, that either party was at the time of the marriage domiciled in England and Wales.

The ground most used by petitioners for annulment of a void marriage is that, at the date of its celebration, one of the parties was already lawfully married. Proof of a prior, subsisting, valid marriage at the date of celebration of the "marriage" under consideration is enough. Unlike the criminal law of bigamy, the state of the parties' knowledge or belief concerning the existence or validity of the prior marriage is irrelevant.

Section 12 of the M.C.A. details the six grounds that are available for declaring a marriage voidable. They are:

(a) non-consummation of marriage due to the incapacity of either party
(b) non-consummation of marriage due to the wilful refusal of the respondent
(c) lack of valid consent to the marriage by either party
(d) that either party was suffering from mental disorder
(e) that the respondent was suffering from VD in a communicable form at the time of the marriage
(f) that the respondent was pregnant by someone other than the petitioner at the time of the marriage.

The grounds most used by petitioners for annulment of a voidable marriage are those relating to non-consummation (which are often pleaded together, in the alternative).

The concept of non-consummation of a marriage is the same, whatever the reason alleged. Consummation is achieved by one act of sexual intercourse after the marriage ceremony. The required act of sexual intercourse must be "ordinary and complete and not partial and imperfect," so that a husband who can sustain an erection for only a very short period of time has been found incapable of consummating his marriage (*W.* v. *W.* (H.L. 1967)). However, lack of ability to ejaculate, withdrawal prior to ejaculation, and the use of a condom have generally been held not to bar a finding of consummation.

If it is alleged that non-consummation is due to incapacity, it does not matter whether the reason for the incapacity is physical or psychological. However, it must be "incurable" in the sense that it is literally incurable, or curable only by an operation that is dangerous, unlikely to succeed or refused by the party suffering the incapacity.

Non-consummation due to incapacity of *either* party is what is required: thus a spouse could petition upon the grounds of his own incapacity.

Knowledge of the incapacity prior to the ceremony, whether it be knowledge of one's own incapacity or that of the other party, is not automatically a bar to a petition but it may well be taken into account under section 13 of the M.C.A. (see below).

If it is alleged that non-consummation is due to wilful refusal, the respondent's decision must be "settled and definite . . . and come to without just excuse" (*Horton* v. *Horton* (H.L. 1947)). Note, the wilful refusal of the *respondent* must be proved before a decree will be granted on this ground.

Bars, Defences and Delays to Nullity

Bars and Defences

As void marriages are marriages that never existed, there can be no bar or defence to a petition for nullity relating to them (save to establish that the ground does not in fact exist).

Section 13 of the M.C.A. deals with bars and defences to petitions alleging marriages to be voidable.

First, a decree must be refused if the respondent satisfies the court that the petitioner by his conduct made the respondent believe that he would not petition for nullity and that it would be unjust to the respondent to grant the decree. The respondent's belief must be reasonably held and the petitioner must have known that he had the grounds to petition for a nullity decree. An example of these principles is to be found in

D. v. D. (H.C. 1979)

> The petitioners agreeing to the adoption of a child by the parties was held to be conduct that led the respondent to believe that the petitioner would not petition for nullity. However, as the respondent wanted the decree too, there was held to be no injustice to her in granting one.

Other defences and bars are detailed in section 13 of the M.C.A. but these do not relate to petitions relying on non-consummation.

Delays

The provisions of the M.C.A., s. 41 (relating to protection for children), apply to all proceedings for nullity, no matter whether it is alleged that the marriage is void or voidable.

DIVORCE REFORM

The UK has one of the highest divorce rates in Europe and it is increasing more rapidly than any other Western country.

The Law Commission published a Discussion Paper in 1988, called "Facing the Future" and a report "The Ground for Divorce" in 1990. In December 1993, Lord Mackay issued a Green Paper based on these proposals and sought consultation. On the basis of the advice received by March 1995 the Government would decide whether or not to embark on legislation.

The basis of the reports is that the law falls far short of its original objectives; it provoked rather than minimised hostility and bitterness and did nothing to save the marriage.

The Commission's proposals in summary are that the breakdown of the marriage would be the only ground for divorce, which either party could initiate by making a formal statement to the Court. However, there could be no divorce within a year, during which period the waiting is to be put to "good and effective" use by considering and reflecting on the marriage and to come to agreement about the consequences of the divorce and the consequences for the children.

It is envisaged that the parties would seek the help of the mediation and conciliation services, though there has been much speculation that these services would be unable to cope with the increased workload without substantial funding (which would appear not to be forthcoming).

The Courts' role would be to make interim orders in the event of lack of agreement but would be bound to grant a decree at the end of the year, subject to certain safeguards. It will have a discretion to postpone the decree if it is desirable in the interests of the child, using its CA powers, if one party lacks capacity, *e.g.* because of mental illness, if a party has delayed furnishing information so that financial arrangements cannot be made, or that the decree would cause grave financial or other hardship, presumably on the terms of existing M.C.A. provisions.

The proposals have the support of the Treasury because of the savings in Legal Aid, and opposition, not only of practitioners but also some members of the Government who see "no fault divorce" being against "the family values" espoused by the Tory party.

2. RIGHTS OF OCCUPATION, FINANCIAL AND PROPERTY AWARDS—SPOUSES

This chapter relates to partners who are or who have been married to each other. Care should be taken to note whether the rights discussed relate only to married partners or to those who have been married as well.

RIGHTS OF OCCUPATION—THE MATRIMONIAL HOMES ACT 1983

Nowadays, many matrimonial homes are owned jointly by the spouses, both as to the legal and beneficial estate. As beneficial owners, both will have the right to occupy the home and as legal owners, both will be able to ensure that their right of occupation is not prejudiced without their consent, for any sale or mortgage requires their signature.

However, some homes are vested solely in the name of one of the parties. At common law, even though the whole of the legal and beneficial estate in the home was vested in the husband, the wife, as wife, had a right to occupy it. However, this right could be defeated by a sale or mortgage to a third party. Further, husbands did not have equal rights in homes belonging to their wives. Finally, even if a spouse had a beneficial interest in the home, if she had no share in the legal estate, it could prove very difficult to protect her interest and the attached right of occupation. The Matrimonial Homes Act 1967 (now 1983) sought to remedy these ills.

By section 1 of the M.H.A., where one spouse (the owning spouse) has a right to occupy property that is or was the matrimonial home and the other (the non-owning spouse) has not, the other is given "statutory rights of occupation" in that property.

Basically, the statutory rights of occupation are:

(a) if the non-owner is in occupation of the home, the right not to be evicted from it without leave of the court

(b) if the non-owner is not in occupation of the home, the right to resume occupation with leave of the court.

It will be noted that a spouse only receives the benefit of the Act if she needs it. A spouse who already has rights of occupation is not entitled to the statutory rights. It is, however, provided that a spouse who has rights of occupation as a result of an interest in the beneficial estate alone (*i.e.* has no interest in the legal estate) is not precluded from being entitled to the statutory rights.

The rights exist until the termination of the marriage, for example by death or divorce (unless extended by the court by application made during the marriage). The rights can also be terminated or restricted by an earlier court order under the M.H.A., s. 1(2). This power is now most often used in cases of domestic violence and will be discussed in Chapter 4.

Creation of rights of occupation as between spouses is not the only objective achieved by the M.H.A. The rights are a charge on the home and can be protected against third parties. The non-owning spouse must register the statutory rights of occupation as either a land charge, class F (for unregistered land) or a notice (for registered land). Such registration can be effected whether or not the non-owning spouse is actually in occupation. If this is done, then any subsequent purchaser for value will take subject to the statutory rights of occupation. It should be noted, however, that he then has the same right as the owning spouse to apply to the court for termination or restriction of the statutory rights of occupation and his own circumstances, as well as the spouses, can be taken into account.

Kashmir Kaur v. *Gill* (C.A. 1988)

The court at first instance refused to enforce a wife's statutory rights of occupation against the purchaser of the home, even though she had registered a notice. In reaching this decision, the court had taken into account the purchaser's circumstances, *i.e.* that he was blind and wanted the property as it was convenient.

Held: the purchaser's circumstances could be taken into account.

FINANCIAL AND PROPERTY AWARDS—THE MATRIMONIAL CAUSES ACT 1973 ANCILLARY TO DECREE PROCEEDINGS

Orders for the Benefit of Spouses

Nature and Duration of Orders

By sections 23 and 24 of the M.C.A. 1973 the court can grant one or more of the following orders against either spouse for the benefit of the other:

(a) a periodical payments order
(b) a secured periodical payments order
(c) an order for lump sum or sums
(d) a transfer of property order
(e) a settlement of property order
(f) a variation of settlement order
(g) an order extinguishing or reducing an interest in a settlement.

None of these orders can be made until a decree of divorce, nullity or judicial separation has been granted. Therefore, if the decree proceedings fail, no order for a spouse can be made under the M.C.A., ss. 23 and 24. All of these orders can be made on the grant of a decree or at any time afterwards, save that a spouse is barred from applying for any of these orders if he or she has remarried prior to the application.

(a) *Periodical payments, secured and unsecured* (M.C.A., s. 23). This is an order that one spouse should pay to the other a specific amount of money periodically, *e.g.* weekly or monthly. If the periodical payment is "secured," this means that it is charged upon a piece of property owned by the paying spouse.

Once made, both forms of periodical payment can last for many years. The death of the payer automatically terminates an unsecured periodical payment: it does not have the same effect on a secured periodical payment, which can go on beyond the death of the payer, the reason being that the property upon which the payment is secured will still be in existence. The remarriage or death of the recipient automatically terminates both forms of periodical payment.

Apart from automatic termination, the court itself has the power to control the duration of both forms of periodical payment. It can order the payments to be made for only a specific length of time and, in addition, can direct that at the end of the specified period the recipient should not be entitled to ask for an extension of the period. (Indeed, the court can order that there should be no periodical payment at all and again, in addition, direct that the applicant should not be entitled to seek such an order at any time in the future.)

(b) *Lump sum* (M.C.A., s. 23). This is an order that one spouse do pay the other a fixed sum or sums of money. It can be provided that the lump sum should be paid in one go or by specified instalments. If the lump sum is ordered to be paid in instalments, the instalments can be secured on some property owned by the payer.

(c) *Transfer of property* (M.C.A., s. 24). This is an order that one spouse transfer to the other property to which the former is entitled. "Property" is not defined in the M.C.A. and section 24 has been used to transfer items such as furniture, jewellery, cars, and other tangible items. It can also cover stocks and shares and, most important, land, including the matrimonial home. Even if the matrimonial home is mortgaged, it can be the subject of a transfer order, and likewise if it is rented (save for a statutory tenancy under the Rent Acts).

(d) *Settlement of property order and variation of settlement order* (M.C.A., s. 24). The former is an order that one spouse settle property to which he is entitled for the benefit of the other. There are no restrictions on the type of settlement that the court can create and again property is widely interpreted.

The variation of settlement order is an order that any ante- or post-nuptial settlement made on the spouses should be varied for their benefit. The phrase "anti- or post-nuptial settlement" conjures up pictures of the sort of arrangements entered into in bygone days by members of the landed gentry on the marriage of their children. Fortunately, the phrase has been widely interpreted and also covers a matrimonial home bought by the parties in their joint names.

By using these two orders the courts have been able to create very sophisticated arrangements designed to meet the needs of individual cases. Three examples will suffice to illustrate how wide ranging the orders can be.

Mesher v. *Mesher* (C.A. 1980)

The home was in joint names, on the usual trust for sale. The court varied the settlement by providing that the property should not be sold until the youngest child of the family reached 17 and in the meantime, the wife should have exclusive rights of occupation.

E. v. *E. (Financial Provision)* (1990)

A wealthy father had created a substantial discretionary trust for his son, his wife and their children, as well as making other provisions for them. The wife was extravagant and profligate and after 10 years of marriage, she left for another man leaving the children with their father. The Court ordered £250,000 be transferred from the trust to the wife and that the father be removed as a trustee of the settlement.

Brooks v. *Brooks* (C.A. 1994)

They married in 1977, in which year the Husband set up a Company which he effectively controlled. In 1980, he established a pension fund with power to surrender a portion of the fund to a spouse and/or dependant. In the divorce proceedings, the trial judge held that the pension fund was a post-nuptial settlement under section 24 of the M.C.A. and varied the terms of the fund for the benefit of the wife. His appeal against the order was dismissed by the Court of Appeal, but they added the condition that any variation must not affect third parties. Although this will limit the effects of this important decision, many personal pension schemes will fall within the ambit of the judgment.

(e) *An order extinguishing or reducing an interest in a settlement* (M.C.A., s. 24). Such an order must relate to an interest of either spouse in an ante- or post-nuptial settlement.

Matters taken into account when making Orders

By section 25(1) of the M.C.A., it is provided that, when deciding whether and how to exercise its powers, the court must consider all the circumstances of the case, but give first consideration to the welfare of any minor children of the family.

In *Suter* v. *Suter and Jones* (C.A. 1986), it was held that giving "first consideration" to the welfare of the children in financial proceedings did not mean that the welfare of the child overrode all other considerations. The courts had to

"consider all the circumstances, . . . always bearing in mind the important consideration of the welfare of the children and then try to attain a financial result which is just as between husband and wife."

The application of this principle is illustrative.

Suter v. Suter and Jones

> The wife had remained in the home with the minor children of the family.
> The husband was content for the home, the main asset of the parties, to
> be transferred to her. The co-respondent lived at the house with the wife,
> but did not contribute anything to the expenses of it. At first instance,
> the court ordered the husband to pay periodical payments to the wife of
> an amount that, together with her wages, was enough to pay all the
> household expenses.
>
> The Court of Appeal held that the judge was wrong. He had made
> the order to ensure the children had a roof over their heads, but this
> was not the only consideration. It would not be unreasonable for the
> co-respondent to make a contribution and the reduced award did more
> justice to the husband.

These provisions remain in force but will be considerably affected by the C.S.A., whereby child maintenance is assessed using
rigid formulae under the jurisdiction of the Child Support Agency,
reducing substantially the jurisdiction of the Courts. Chapter 4
contains a more detailed discussion of these provisions.

Section 25(2) of the M.C.A. directs the Court to have regard
to the following list of factors when exercising their powers to
make financial provision for a spouse.

(a) *Income, earning capacity, property and other financial resources.* Prima
facie, the court must have regard to all of the income and capital
of both parties, including any they are likely to have in the
foreseeable future. So far as income is concerned, this will include
both earned and unearned income, *e.g.* wages, salary, profits from
a business, bonuses, commissions and overtime, dividends and
interest from investments and pensions. So far as capital is concerned this will include all land, investments, cash, and personal
possessions even if obtained as a bequest or gift or meant for a
specific purpose, such as compensation. Its source or purpose will
be borne in mind, however, and the court will not always make
an order that divests the owner of any benefit.

A party's earning capacity is also a resource (including any
that he is likely to have in the foreseeable future) and it is also
specifically provided that the court should have regard to any
increase in earning capacity which it is reasonable to expect a
party to take steps to acquire. If the court thinks that such a
party is being unreasonable then they can attribute "lost" income
to that party. Obviously, the court will take into account such
matters as job or overtime availability, the efforts made to find
employment or better employment, the availability of retraining

or refresher courses and the feasibility of a party undergoing such courses.

Leadbeater v. Leadbeater (1985)

> Wife, aged 47, had been a secretary before marriage but the Court thought it unreasonable for her to learn new skills. However, she could have worked longer hours at her part-time job as a receptionist and her notional earnings were set at £2,550, as opposed to her actual income of £1,700.

Often the applicant is in receipt of state benefits. Do these count as a resource? If they are not means tested—*e.g.* child benefit—and thus will be paid whether or not a financial award is made in favour of the applicant, then they count as a resource, to be taken into account when assessing the award. However, if the state benefit is means tested—*e.g.* income support, family credit—this is not taken into account as a resource as a general rule. Respondents to financial applications are not generally permitted to argue that the applicant can claim a state benefit if no (or a small) financial award were made against them (but see *e.g. Delaney* v. *Delaney* (C.A. 1990)).

One or both of the parties may have a new partner, either as a new spouse or as a cohabitee, by the time the court is deciding what financial orders to make after decree. If such a new partner has their own income or capital, then such resources cannot be taken as being the resources of the party with whom they are living (but see below).

(b) *Financial needs, obligations and responsibilities.* Again, prima facie, the court must have regard to all such matters, including those which the parties are likely to have in the foreseeable future. This obviously includes living expenses, *e.g.* mortgage or rent, council tax, water rates, electricity and gas, food and clothing. Regard will also be had to income tax and national insurance contributions, to union dues and pension contributions and to the cost of travelling to and from work.

The parties will be expected to be reasonable when giving evidence of such matters and not to inflate their needs in the hope that the court will take the view that there is less available for division or more needed. Thus constant wining and dining, expensive holidays abroad and powerful and expensive motor cars would not be regarded as a part of the needs of an ordinary person. Even some of the matters that are referred to above, *e.g.* pension contributions, could be disregarded as unreasonable if their size made them so in the circumstances.

Any liabilities of a capital nature must also be taken into account. For example, when assessing the value of the matrimonial home, the outstanding mortgage, if any, must be deducted. Liabilities, such as a bank overdraft, personal or for business purposes, must be taken into account. Tax that will have to be paid on the realisation of investments must not be forgotten.

As was mentioned above, by the time the court decides what orders to make after decree, either or both of the parties may have a new partner, and that new partner may have an income of his own. While such a resource is not a resource of the party to the proceedings, the fact that his partner has an income will be taken into account to the extent that the partner contributes to, and thereby reduces, the needs of the party. The position becomes more complex when the new partner can afford to contribute but does not do so. Sometimes, such a partner will be taken as contributing a reasonable amount. As has been seen, in *Suter* v. *Suter and Jones*, the court made an order that left the wife without enough money to meet all her needs, assuming the co-respondent would start contributing to the household expenses.

On the other hand, the new partner may, reasonably, have no income or capital to contribute. In such cases, the question then is whether the party to the proceedings is entitled to have taken into account as an obligation or responsibility the needs of his new partner. Such cases usually arise where the husband has a new partner, by whom he has children or who already has children of her own. While such children are not the first consideration of the court (see above), they, and their mother, are to be seen as the responsibility of the husband. But note the entirely different approach of the C.S.A. (see Chapter 4).

(c) *Standard of living.* The court must take into account the standard of living enjoyed by the family before the breakdown of the marriage. In some cases the court will exercise its powers so that the marriage breakdown will have the least possible effect on the standard of living of the parties.

(d) *Age of the parties and duration of the marriage.* The age of the parties must be taken into account by the court and can be relevant for several reasons. For example, the age of a person may affect promotion prospects or, more radically, whether or not

a job can be found at all. See *M.* v. *M.* (*Financial Provision*) (1987).
It will also affect the ability to raise finance by way of mortgage
and will affect the type and size of pension that can be bought.

The duration of the marriage must also be taken into account
by the court. There is no definition of what is "long" or "short",
but a "short marriage" is usually taken to mean one of only a
very few years. Generally, the parties to a short marriage will
have less claim on each other than those who have been married
for some appreciable period, on the basis that they will have
changed their positions less drastically.

Attar v. *Attar* (1985)

> Before marriage to a multi-millionaire, she had been an air hostess earn-
> ing £15,000 p.a. The marriage only lasted six months: she was awarded
> a lump sum of £30,000.

But even a short marriage can produce children, and short marriages between older couples can still mean a change in their
positions, for example the loss of pension rights previously accrued.

(e) *Disabilities.* The court must take into account any physical or
mental disability of either of the parties to the marriage. Obviously,
the needs of such a person, even if only in financial terms, will
be special.

(f) *Contributions to the welfare of the family.* It is specifically provided
that this includes any contribution made by looking after the
home or caring for the family. Thus the wife, who gives up her
job and contributes nothing to the family in hard cash, but is the
home maker and child rearer, has the value of such activities
recognised.

(g) *Conduct.* The court must take into account the conduct of each
of the parties if it would be "inequitable to disregard it." This
is obviously a very vague principle and gives considerable discretion to the courts.

The principle was introduced by the M.F.P.A. but this is not
to say that the conduct of the parties was irrelevant to the exercise
of the courts powers prior to 1984. However, in *Wachtel* v. *Wachtel*
(C.A. 1973), Lord Denning M.R. had said that the courts should
only take conduct into account where it was "obvious and gross."
According to this formula, there had to be a certain amount of

extremity, which in past cases has included such conduct as stabbing or shooting one's spouse.

The case of *Kyte* v. *Kyte* (C.A. 1987) contains an interpretation of the principle. The Court of Appeal approved the District Judge's approach, when he asked himself the rhetorical question

> "whether a right thinking member of society, faced with the conclusions (on the facts) I have reached, would say that the matters of conduct were such as to reduce or extinguish the wife's entitlement?"

Further, in *K*. v. *K*. (H.C. 1990), the court stated that:

> "the court is entitled to look at the whole of the picture, including the conduct during the marriage and after the marriage, which may or may not have contributed to the breakdown . . . or which in some other way makes it inequitable to ignore the conduct of each of the parties."

It would still seem, however, that an extremity of conduct is required. In the following four cases, the spouses' claim for ancillary relief was affected by their conduct.

Kyte v. *Kyte*

> The wife behaved callously when the husband, a manic depressive, made two suicide attempts. On the first, she was present and only called assistance at the last moment: on the second she encouraged him, giving him the tablets and alcohol with which to kill himself and jeering him when he failed to carry out his intentions. The court found as a fact that the wife wanted the husband dead so that she could inherit his money, and share it with her lover.

Evans v. *Evans* (C.A. 1989)

> The wife had been convicted of soliciting others to murder the husband.

K. v. *K*. (1990)

> The husband had a personality disorder and had had a drink problem. He had been unemployed for a long time and had indulged in "disagreeable behaviour," including neglecting the home and it ultimately being repossessed and sold. The court regarded his situation as largely "self-inflicted."

Leadbeater v. *Leadbeater* (1985)

> The conduct of both parties cancelled each other out so that it ceased to be an issue in the case.

Conduct, even if relevant, is only one of the factors that the court has to consider and, as a result, the applicant may still receive some award. In fact, Mrs. Kyte still received a lump sum, as did Mr. K.

(h) *The value of any lost benefit.* In the nullity and divorce cases (but not judicial separation) the court must also take into account the value of any benefit the parties lose the chance of acquiring as a result of a decree, *e.g.* pension rights.

In addition to the list of factors just discussed, there are further considerations for the courts. There are contained in section 25A of the M.C.A., a section that was introduced by the M.F.P.A. and which embodies the policy decision that the objective for the exercise of the court's financial powers should be to make the parties financially independent of each other. This principle is often referred to as the clean break principle. It applies only where the court has granted a decree of divorce or nullity.

By section 25A(1), the court is placed under a duty to consider whether it is appropriate to make orders that will terminate the parties' financial obligations towards each other as soon after the decree as the court thinks is just and reasonable. The court must therefore consider whether it should make use of the powers it has to make no orders for continuing provision (primarily periodical payments) and to ensure that no future applications are made. Only if such a situation is created can the parties be said to be truly independent of each other.

Section 25A(2) creates a secondary obligation on the court. If it has decided that an order for periodical payments should be made (thus not ordering a clean break), then it must consider whether to order that the payments should cease after a specified period, a period designed to permit an adjustment to financial independence without undue hardship.

It must be emphasised that the court has no duty to *order* a clean break, immediate or delayed: it has a duty to consider whether it *should* order a clean break in every case where it was asked to exercise its financial powers on divorce (or nullity).

The Exercise of the Powers

The first point to make is that the court can make one or more of the orders specified in the M.C.A., ss. 23 and 24. In other words, by a judicious combination of orders drawn from both sections, the court can create a "package deal" that is suitable for the particular couple. It is therefore somewhat unrealistic to consider when any particular order will be made, in isolation: when circumstances permit, a generous periodical payments order might be reflected in the capital award or disposition of the home, and vice versa. Further, orders may be made in favour of both of the parties: for example, if circumstances permit, the court may prefer to order the transfer of the home outright to the wife coupled with an order that she pay the husband a lump sum, instead of one of the more complex property adjustment orders. This must be borne in mind during the following discussion.

(a) *The clean break.* Parliament could have provided that a clean break should be ordered in every case immediately. It did not, thus showing that, although the clean break is to be the financial objective on marriage breakdown, it is also thought that a clean break will not always be appropriate. Further, Parliament has left it up to the courts to decide the sort of cases in which clean breaks are appropriate, giving them no further guidance than the principle and factors previously discussed.

Prior to the C.S.A., the most problematical cases concerned women with children or women who had cared for children. Their commitments often took them out of the job market or gave them little chance of entering it. Without periodical payments, many suffered a reduction in living standards. However, practitioners realised that if the wife was to have to rely on state benefits, then income support would meet the mortgage repayments. Thus, a clean break could be effected by transferring the matrimonial home to her and the State would foot the mortgage bill. This popular clean break agreement has suffered substantive setbacks in the last few years, both from the C.S.A. and the Social Security legislation.

Under the C.S.A., the levels of child maintenance now preclude such arrangements. Indeed, in many cases, the increased assessments take the parent with care outside income support. As it is not possible to "contract out" of the C.S.A., any clean break settlement would have to be arrived at after taking the maintenance assessments into account, making such arrangements where there are minor children of the family highly unlikely in all but a handful of cases.

Even if there are no children, or a formula can be found allowing for child support, one has now to consider the provisions of sections 107 and 108 of the Social Security Administration Act 1992 and the Income Support (Liable Relative) Regulations 1990. There are long standing regulations permitting the D.S.S. to recover income support payments from liable relatives, but that power ceased on a decree absolute. This is no longer the case and the Department can effectively re-write a clean break settlement by proceeding against the ex-husband whenever the ex-wife and or children become dependent on income support.

The recent legislation is clearly in conflict with the spirit of section 25A of the M.C.A.

In cases where a clean break may still be an appropriate option, the Courts have to consider whether or not it is acceptable for a woman to remain financially dependent on her ex-spouse indefinitely.

Waterman v. *Waterman* (C.A. 1989)

Wife was granted periodical payments order for five years, even though she had a five year old child. Judge at first instance refused to extend it. Court of Appeal said she could apply for an extension at the end of the period but she would still have to make out a case.

Ashley v. *Blackman* (1988)

A clean break was imposed where husband had limited means and wife, who was on state benefits, would not suffer as a result of the loss of periodical payments. The Court said it had to consider the two policies of clean break and protecting state funds and strike "whatever balance . . . between them that the requirements of justice in the particular circumstances appear to dictate".

Lump sum compensation is usually only available to the more wealthy families. Most husbands do not have substantial free capital available: if they do, what should they pay?

Gojkovic v. *Gojkovic* (C.A. 1990)

He had developed a chain of hotels and property businesses worth £4 million. His wife had made "exceptional contributions" in helping to run the hotels. She was awarded £1 million to enable her to start up her own hotel business.

Duxbury v. *Duxbury* (1990)

> Millionaire husband ordered to pay a lump sum sufficient to produce an income of £28,000 per year, which the Court felt was a reasonable amount to support a luxurious standard of living.

(b) *Income Awards.* In *Wachtel* v. *Wachtel* (C.A. 1973) Lord Denning M.R. stated that as a starting point the wife should "receive one third of the joint earnings and assets". The parties incomes from all sources are added together and divided by three. The resulting figure is the amount of income the wife should have. If her own income does not add up to this figure, then it is to be made up by a periodical payments order from the husband. This has become known as the "One third rule" for obvious reasons. However, the use of the word rule does an injustice to Lord Denning who did stress the principle should be a starting point only. Once a figure for periodical payments is arrived at using the one third rule, the Court then considers whether it is appropriate.

The rule has been in and out of favour during the eighties. *Stockford* v. *Stockford* (C.A. 1981) was disapproving, *Potter* v. *Potter* (C.A. 1982) stated that it was inappropriate in cases involving capital distribution but it was back in favour (at least as a starting point) by 1986 in *Bullock* v. *Bullock* and *Dew* v. *Dew*.

It is still quite widely used, possibly because no-one has found a better alternative. It must be borne in mind, however, that the one third approach is not applicable where the parties are very rich or very poor. The much higher levels of child maintenance brought in by the C.S.A. are likely to have an impact as well, because the maintenance assessment includes an amount for the carer. A one third-based periodical payment on top of child maintenance would penalise the payer.

A more sophisticated principle for calculating periodical payments is known as the "Net Effect Method" and was first fully stated by Ormrod J. in *Stockford* v. *Stockford* (1981). The Court arrive at a proposed order (whether by using the one third rule or by any other means) and then calculate what the parties respective positions would be if the proposed order were made. The calculations must include all income relevant for section 25 of the M.C.A., bearing in mind the reduction of the payer's income by the proposed order, and takes account of reasonable expenditure that the parties have, particularly tax and expenses for earning it, but also including revised housing and living costs. What is left is the respective spendable incomes which can then be adjusted through the order to achieve the result which the Court thinks is most appropriate.

It should also be noted that the Court will not generally make a periodical payments order which will reduce the payer's income below "subsistence level" (*see Allen* v. *Allen* (1986)). Subsistence level is the amount which the D.S.S. would find the payer entitled to if he were on income support and housing benefit.

(c) *Capital awards.* The one-third rule, as first stated in *Wachtel* v. *Wachtel,* applied not only to the calculation of the wife's periodical payments but also to her capital claims. However, it was soon appreciated that there were many cases in which the one-third rule could not be usefully used even as the starting point it was meant to be.

The main problem experienced in applying the one-third rule is with cases where the parties' only or main asset is the matrimonial home. Of course, the bulk of cases coming before the courts, where the parties have any assets at all, consist of precisely these cases. The one-third rule treats all assets as if they were cash assets or assets that can readily be converted into cash. Of course, a home can be so realised, but if it is, and if the wife is to be given only one-third of the proceeds this will usually not be sufficient to enable the wife to rehouse herself. If in addition, the wife has children living with her or has spent many years in child rearing and therefore has little or no ability to work or obtain a mortgage, the result of applying the one-third rule in cases where the only asset is the home is that the wife (and the children) are homeless. The courts soon realised that, in some cases, the home had to be regarded as a means of providing accommodation for the wife (and children).

The result has been the development of sophisticated property adjustment orders using the court's powers to settle or vary an existing settlement of property. Typical is the case of

Mesher v. *Mesher* (1973)

The home was in joint names on the usual trust for sale. There were no other assets. An application of the one-third rule would have indicated no capital award to the wife, as her joint interest in the home already exceeded her entitlement to one-third. However, the court were concerned to ensure that the nine year old child of the marriage should be accommodated, so provided that the trust for sale should be varied and that the home should not be sold until the child reached 17 or further order.

Not surprisingly, this type of order became called "the Mesher order" and was extremely popular in the Seventies.

The advantage of the "Mesher" was also its disadvantage: it put off the evil day when the wife (and possibly children) are put on the street. By 1978, particularly in *Martin* v. *Martin*, the Court of Appeal were critical of the universal use of such orders. It was pointed out that children do not always leave home at 17, that even when they do, the wife has to find somewhere to live and she will then (in all probability) be in her forties with negligible employment prospects (concerns, incidentally, expressed a decade or so before the recent recession and the current high levels of unemployment).

In *Clutton* v. *Clutton* (C.A. 1991) the Court said that if there was doubt that the wife could rehouse herself when the charge took effect, then an order should not be made. But it was still the best solution

> "where the family assets are amply sufficient to provide both parties with a roof over their heads if the matrimonial home were sold, but nevertheless the interests of the children require that they remain in the home. In such a case, it may be just and sensible to postpone the sale until the children have left home".

An alternative is the so-called "Martin" order named after the case mentioned above. Like "Mesher" orders the house is settled on the spouses on trust for sale, but the contingencies are different.

Harvey v. *Harvey* (C.A. 1982)

The home was in the husband's name but he had found alternative accommodation. They had been married for 19 years, there were six children, two still minors. It was ordered that the house be transferred into joint names, with the equity held one third to him and two thirds to her but there would be no sale until the wife died, remarried, voluntarily left the property or became dependent on another man. She was required to pay the mortgage and an occupational rent once this was discharged.

Clutton v. *Clutton* (1991)

The contingent events were death, remarriage or co-habitation. The wife's objection that she would "be spied upon by her husband" was outweighed by the potential bitterness of the husband if she soon remarried or co-habited and still occupied the house.

But what of the cases where the matrimonial home is not the only or main asset? The husband may be sufficiently wealthy for the court to give the wife a capital award outright that ensures that she will have reasonable housing and perhaps more too. In these cases, the one-third rule has had a chequered career, sometimes being in favour and sometimes not. A recent comment is to be found in *Dew* v. *Dew*, where Lincoln J. stated:

> "the fraction can serve as a starting point from which one can take one's bearing in one's journey through the provisions of section 25 . . ."

In fact, in *Dew* v. *Dew*, the considerations of the M.C.A., s. 25 persuaded the court "to leave far behind" the figure produced by the application of the one-third rule. The wife was awarded the sum of £135,000 over a period of two years, a figure that was about one-half of that arrived at by applying the one-third rule. This was despite the fact that she had contributed substantially to the running of the family business over a 14 year marriage and was prepared to give up her rights to maintenance. But, she had already rehoused herself and a substantial proportion of his wealth was tied up in shares that were not immediately realisable or not realisable at all.

This case also illustrates the principle that when making capital awards the court will take into account the realisability of the parties assets. Similarly, if in response to a court order, a realisation of assets, *e.g.* the value of a business would have adverse effects, *e.g.* the collapse of the business such an order would not be made.

It is also worth placing the one-third rule in its context. In *Wachtel* v. *Wachtel*, the court was considering a long marriage and the wife was claiming periodical payments as well.

Orders for the Benefit of Children

Children of the family can have the same types of orders made in their favour, against either of the parties of the marriage, as can the parties themselves. For a discussion of this, see Chapter 4.

Other Powers:

Brief mention must be made of the court's powers to:

(a) order a spouse to pay maintenance pending suit to the other, a temporary periodical payment that ceases on decree absolute (M.C.A., s. 22)

(b) order a sale of property when it has made any of the orders in sections 23 or 24 of the M.C.A., save for unsecured periodical payments (M.C.A., s. 24A).

FINANCIAL AWARDS—THE DOMESTIC PROCEEDINGS AND MAGISTRATES' COURT ACT 1978

It may be the case that a party to a marriage may need some form of financial order against the other but cannot or does not wish to issue decree proceedings. The D.P.M.C.A. is one of several statutes that give the courts power to order financial relief without the necessity of first obtaining any order relating to the status of the marriage itself. Three different situations are covered by the Act.

Sections 1 and 2 of the D.P.M.C.A.

Although the applicant is not seeking any form of decree, he still has to establish one of the grounds as set out in section 1 before the court can grant him one of the financial orders set out in section 2. The grounds are:

(a) that the respondent has failed to provide reasonable maintenance for the applicant

(b) that the respondent has failed to provide or make proper contribution towards the reasonable maintenance of a child of the family

(c) that the respondent has behaved in such a way that the applicant cannot reasonably be expected to live with him

(d) that the respondent has deserted the applicant.

It will be noted that these grounds bear some similarity to the facts that evidence irretrievable breakdown of marriage, but they are not identical. The concepts of behaviour and desertion are exactly the same under the D.P.M.C.A. as they are under the M.C.A., but there is no adultery or separation ground. It is thought that the adultery of the respondent could be used as one of the elements to establish behaviour. On the other hand, the D.P.M.C.A., s. 1, contains a ground not available in divorce proceedings, that of failure to provide reasonable maintenance.

There is no definition of the term "reasonable maintenance" in the Act: clearly, the court would have to take into account the parties respective financial positions at least in making their determination.

Once the applicant has proved one of the grounds, the court has the power to make one or more of the orders as set out in section 2. They are:

(a) that the respondent should pay periodical payments to the applicant and/or a child of the family.

(b) that the respondent should pay a lump sum to the applicant and or a child of the family, such lump sum not to exceed £1,000.

The payments for children can be ordered to be made direct to them or to some third party for their benefit.

It will be noted that the court has a far more limited range of orders available to it under the D.P.M.C.A. than it does under the M.C.A., ss. 23 and 24.

If the applicant fails to prove one of the grounds all is not lost: the court still has the power to make the orders for the benefit of children, but the advent of the C.S.A. is likely to make these provisions redundant.

Orders for periodical payments cease on the death of the payer. Orders for periodical payments to a spouse cease on her remarriage. The rules for the cessation of periodical payments for children on their reaching a certain age are the same as under the M.C.A. (see above). Further, orders for periodical payments that are payable to a spouse, either for herself or a child, cease if the parties continue to cohabit or resume cohabitation after the making of the order for a period or periods exceeding six months.

Once a ground is proved, the court has to decide whether to make any order at all. Again, under the D.P.M.C.A., the welfare of any minor child of the family, while a minor, is the court's first consideration. Then, by section 3, the court is given a list of factors to take into account. For both spouse and child orders, the factors are virtually identical to those listed in the M.C.A., s. 25(2)(3)(4). What should be carefully noted is that under the D.P.M.C.A., the court has no duty to consider imposing a clean break upon even the parties and cannot do so even if the parties consent.

FINANCIAL AWARDS—SECTION 27 OF THE MATRIMONIAL CAUSES ACT 1973

The court can grant periodical payments, secured or unsecured, and lump sum for spouses and children of the family on proof simply of failure to provide reasonable maintenance. Again, section 27 provides a means of obtaining orders for financial relief without issuing decree proceedings. However, it is another provision that is little used, despite the fact that the range of orders available is wider than under the D.P.M.C.A.

FINANCIAL AND PROPERTY AWARDS—SECTION 15 OF THE CHILDREN ACT 1989

Section 15 of the CA provides for the grant of a range of financial orders for the benefit of a child. The applicant must be the parent (or guardian) of the child and the orders can be made against a parent.

It must be stressed that the availability of these orders is not dependent upon the parties to the application being married to one another: it is dependent upon parenthood. Nevertheless, married parents may wish to make use of the CA, s. 15, which is yet another provision whereby the court can grant financial relief without the necessity of the parties first issuing decree proceedings.

Further, the term "parent" includes ex-spouses in relation to whom the child is a child of the family.

The nature of the orders possible under the CA, s. 15, is discussed in Chapter 3.

By now, it will be appreciated that there are a number of jurisdictions available for the grant of financial and property awards, all bearing a similarity to each other but all having significant differences. These are not completely arbitrary; some rationale can be found when it is remembered that different situations are being catered for.

3. RIGHTS OF OCCUPATION, FINANCIAL AND PROPERTY AWARDS—UNMARRIED PARTNERS AND SPOUSES WHO ARE NOT DIVORCING

The previous chapter considered property rights of husband and wife in matrimonial proceedings.

This chapter relates to spouses who do not seek a decree and to partners who have never been married to each other.

In relation to the former, the following rights are important where divorce is not contemplated, or where a spouse has become insolvent or died. With cohabitees, the M.C.A. does not apply so these are their only rights with regard to joint property. The only difference between the two classes is that cohabitees have to prove to the Court that they had a "settled" relationship which was intended to be permanent; perhaps ironic in view of the high divorce rate amongst married couples where such intention is taken for granted!

Establishing a Trust

When dealing with land, there will always be documentary evidence as to ownership—the title deeds. It may be that both parties own the legal estate or only one. In some cases of joint legal ownership the deeds will also spell out the ownership of the equitable (beneficial) estate. More rarely, there may be a separate declaration of trust document that does this. In these cases, in the absence of fraud, the provisions for the ownership of the home are conclusive: extrinsic evidence to challenge the details in the deeds cannot be adduced (*Goodman* v. *Gallant* ((C.A. 1986)). The result is that the ownership dispute has been resolved solely by consideration of the title deeds.

However, in some cases of joint ownership the beneficial interests are not spelt out. Here there is a rebuttable presumption that the legal owners are each entitled to an equal share of the beneficial estate. Further, the legal estate in the home may be vested in the sole name of one of the cohabitees. Here, there is a rebuttable presumption that the beneficial interest also belongs exclusively to that person. In both these situations therefore, consideration of the title deeds alone will not necessarily provide the answer to an ownership dispute. Extrinsic evidence to rebut the presumptions can be adduced, evidence of the existence of a trust behind the deeds.

Standard works on Equity categorise trusts into four types: express, resulting, implied and constructive. Express trusts, those created by the express declaration of the person in whom the property is vested, are not common in the family context. The traditional distinctions between the other three are of little relevance: not only do the standard works on Equity fail to agree on categorisation but the family law judges have often shown a disregard for it. What is of relevance is the circumstances in which the court will accept that a trust has arisen, whether resulting, implied or constructive.

The principles for resolving the ownership dispute will be discussed as if the property were in the sole name of the man and the woman were claiming a share, but it must be remembered that they are equally applicable where the property is vested in the sole name of the woman and where the property is in joint names, but the applicant is claiming more than the presumed half share.

Payment Towards the Purchase Price

Where A. provides the whole or part of the purchase price for property that is conveyed into B.'s name, there is a rebuttable presumption that A. intended that he, A., should benefit and that B. should hold the property on trust for A., either exclusively or in part, *i.e.* the beneficial estate "results" in whole or in part, to A. The trust is therefore known as a resulting trust. A recent case which concerned the use of this concept is *Sekhon* v. *Alissa* (H.C. 1989).

The concept of resulting trust is rarely directly applicable in the family context because usually the home is not purchased outright but by way of a mortgage. However, the influence of the doctrine will be seen in the principles next discussed.

A Common Intention Inferred from Conduct

The starting point is the body of principles stated in two cases in the House of Lords, *Pettit* v. *Pettit* (H.L. 1969) and *Gissing* v. *Gissing* (H.L. 1970). Both cases concerned a spouse who did not have an interest in the legal estate in the home claiming to be entitled to a beneficial interest by way of trust. Virtually all the Lords, in both cases specifically stated that a trust could arise where both parties had intended it should: the court should look for "a common intention that both parties should be beneficially entitled" (hereafter referred to as "the common intent"). Further, it would seem that the majority in both cases felt that it was necessary to be able to infer the common intention, as distinct from imputing to the parties what a reasonable person would have intended in the circumstances.

However, proof of conduct from which the court can infer the common intent is not sufficient. The woman must also prove that she has "acted to her detriment or significantly altered her position in reliance on the common intent" before a trust in her favour will arise. The necessity for such conduct was first clearly stated in *Grant* v. *Edwards* (C.A. 1986), but has been confirmed by the Lords in *Lloyd's Bank PLC* v. *Rosset* (H.L. 1990).

Therefore, before such a trust can be established, the court will scrutinise the parties' conduct for two reasons: the first, to ascertain whether there was the common intent; the second, to ascertain whether the woman has acted upon it. The crucial questions are then seen to be what sort of conduct will give rise to the inference of common intent and what sort of conduct will show that the woman has acted upon it?

The most recent and authoritative statements on these issues are to be found in the leading judgment of Lord Bridge in *Lloyd's Bank PLC* v. *Rosset*. Express discussions between the parties as to their interests in the property do not amount to conduct from which a common intent can be inferred: presumably, nothing needs to be *inferred* from express discussions. What is looked for are:

> "direct contributions to the purchase price by the partner who is not the legal owner, whether initially or by payment of mortgage instalments." These "will readily justify the inference necessary to the creation of a constructive trust. But . . . it is at least extremely doubtful whether anything less will do."

Lord Bridge made no comment on the sort of conduct needed to show that the woman has acted to her detriment in relying upon the common intent. Arguably, he did not need to. If she has made direct contributions to the purchase price of the property, then this will surely be taken as her having acted to her detriment in relying upon the common intent. If she has not, apparently, she will not be able to satisfy the court that an inference of common intent should be drawn and her claim will fail at this point.

An Express Agreement

Where there is evidence of the parties having entered into "an agreement, arrangement or understanding that the property is to be shared beneficially" then, in some circumstances, the court will hold that a trust has arisen. The finding of such an agreement, etc., can only be based on evidence of "express discussions" between the parties, however "imperfectly remembered and however imprecise the terms." All the above principles are stated in the judgment of Lord Bridge in *Lloyd's Bank PLC* v. *Rosset.*

However, proving such an agreement, etc., is not the end of the matter. Again, the woman must also show that she "has acted to her detriment or significantly altered her position in reliance on the agreement" before the court will hold that a trust in her favour has arisen.

Two points should be noted concerning this type of trust. First, it can be distinguished from an express trust, which does not require an *agreement* between the parties, nor the woman having "acted to her detriment." Secondly, it can be distinguished from a trust arising from the common intention of the parties, because the court does not *infer* an agreement: direct evidence of it must be present.

Obviously, again the crucial issue is the sort of conduct that is required before, for this type of trust, the woman will be held to have acted to her detriment. On this issue, Lord Bridge commented that such conduct could fall

> "far short of such conduct as would *by itself* have supported the claim (that a trust had arisen) in the absence of an express representation by the male partner that she was to have . . . an interest."

In other words, where there is evidence of an express agreement between the parties, and there is thus no need to persuade the court to draw an inference of common intent from the parties' conduct, the woman need not show direct contributions to the purchase price to prove that she has acted to her detriment in reliance on the agreement. So, what does she have to show?

Lord Bridge cited two cases in which the woman had been held, in his view, correctly, to have a beneficial interest in property vested in the sole name of her male partner: *Grant* v. *Edwards* and *Eves* v. *Eves* (C.A. 1975). In both, there was evidence of an express agreement that the woman should have a share. In *Grant* v. *Edwards*, the woman had paid the general household bills, as well as for the parties' food. In *Eves* v. *Eves*, the woman had made no financial contribution at all, but had laboured extensively on improvements to the property. In *Grant* v. *Edwards*, the woman's contribution was described variously as

> "referable to the acquisition of the property" — (in the sense that the man could not have afforded to pay the mortgage on the property without the woman paying the other bills) and "conduct on which the woman could not reasonably have been expected to embark unless she was to have an interest in the house."

In *Eves* v. *Eves*, the woman's contribution was described as "much more than many wives would do."

Comment: This has been an area of law that has seen immense development of principles over the last 35 years. The Lords decisions of *Pettit* v. *Pettit* and *Gissing* v. *Gissing* were the first to overtly state the need for the woman to show a common intent; *Grant* v. *Edwards*, the first to overtly state the need for the woman to show that she had acted to her detriment in relying upon it; *Lloyd's Bank* v. *Rosset* draws a clear distinction between trusts arising from express discussions and trusts arising from inferences drawn from other types of conduct.

Thus, it is extremely difficult, if not impossible, to synthesise all cases in this area. At best, it involves "reinterpreting" earlier cases in the light of, in particular, the judgment of Lord Bridge in *Lloyd's Bank PLC* v. *Rosset* (with which all other Lords agreed).

What is a further matter for concern is Lord Bridge's statement that, where it was necessary for the court to infer a common intent from the conduct of the parties (because there was no evidence of an express agreement), this could only be done from evidence of *direct* payments to the purchase price.

This particular principle seems extremely difficult to reconcile with earlier authorities. In these, arguably, and with respect to Lord Bridge, some types of *indirect* financial contributions have been held to be sufficient to raise the inference of common intent and not just been seen as evidence of the woman having acted to her detriment in relying upon express discussions. See, for example, the statements of Lord Diplock in *Gissing* v. *Gissing*, and those of Lords Justices Fox and May in *Burns* v. *Burns* (C.A. 1984).

Further, if Lord Bridge's statements represent an accurate interpretation of the law, this means that, in cases where the parties do not expressly discuss their intentions as to the ownership of the property, domestic arrangements as to who pays what, possibly made only for the convenience of the parties, will dictate the outcome of an ownership dispute.

Finally, from what has been said, it will be appreciated that a woman who has no financial resources of her own to contribute, whether it be directly or indirectly, is at a severe disadvantage. This will often arise as a result of her having stayed at home to raise a family. For a married but divorcing woman, this contribution must be taken into account under the M.C.A., s. 25, when assessing what property rights she should have: outside the M.C.A., this contribution is ignored in assessing what property rights she does have.

Quantification of Beneficial Interests under a Trust

In the past few years, there have been more and more cases concerning the quantification of shares. The issue seems to have been specifically addressed first in the case of *Turton* v. *Turton* (C.A. 1987), which confirmed the use of property law principles to resolve it.

Where the case concerns a resulting trust, the shares are determined in proportion to the parties' financial contributions. This is well-established law and a demonstration of its use can be found in *Sekhon* v. *Alissa*.

Where the case concerns a trust arising from an express agreement of the parties or a trust arising from their common intent, as inferred from their conduct, the shares are determined by reference to that agreement or, if there is none, their common intent (*Stokes* v. *Anderson* (C.A. 1991)). Where there is no agreement, the court is entitled to look at:

> "all the circumstances surrounding the acquisition of the property, things said and done then and subsequently" including "their respective financial contributions to the purchase price" *B.* v. *B.* (H.C. 1988).

> "the contributions which in total each had . . . made. Those contributions would include, in addition to the original contribution, sums contributed to discharge of the . . . mortgage and the cost of capital improvements." *Passee* v. *Passee* (C.A. 1988).

In *Risch* v. *McFee* (C.A. 1991), the woman made a number of financial contributions to the purchase of the property, which was vested in the man's sole name. The first of these was a loan and was ignored by the first instance judge when deciding that she had a beneficial interest. However, he took it into account when deciding the *extent* of her interest and this was confirmed on appeal.

In *Stokes* v. *Anderson*, the court stated that having considered "all payments and acts done" by the woman, there was no "practicable alternative" when determining her share to deciding what was "fair".

Further, it is clear from a number of cases that the quantification of shares need not be agreed or commonly intended at the date of acquisition of the property. The parties can simply agree or commonly intend to leave open this issue, to be decided later on in their relationship (see *Passee* v. *Passee* and *Stokes* v. *Anderson*).

It is suggested that some of the passages quoted above, particularly the reference in *Stokes* v. *Anderson* to "fairness," show that the principles concerning the quantification of shares have not yet been fully tied into the strait-jacket of strict property law.

Proprietary Estoppel

Estoppel is the principle that prevents a person from exercising or asserting his legal rights and usually the principle can only be pleaded in the defence of an action to exercise or assert those rights. Proprietary estoppel however can also be used to assert contrary rights. Obviously, the circumstances in which such a situation will be recognised by the law are rigorously defined. They have been fully discussed in *Coombes* v. *Smith* (H.C. 1987), where the court stated that a claim to a share in the beneficial interest of property based upon proprietary estoppel would only succeed if the claimant could show:

  (a) that she had made a mistake as to her legal rights in the property
  (b) that she had spent money or done some other act as a result of that mistake
  (c) that the defendant knew of his own rights in the property inconsistent with those she thought she had
  (d) that he knew of her mistaken belief
  (e) that he encouraged her to act as mentioned above.

(It will be seen that the concept of proprietary estoppel has, of late, heavily influenced the development of the trust principles discussed above.)

The application of the concept can be illustrated by comparing two cases.

Coombes v. Smith

The relationship had lasted some ten years during which time the plaintiff had borne a child. The home was vested in the sole name of the defendant although the plaintiff had paid for central heating to be installed and for some decorating. Twice the plaintiff had asked for her name to be included on the title deeds and twice the defendant had refused, telling her that she "was not to worry about her future."

Held: the plaintiff had not established that she was entitled to a share in the home on the basis of proprietary estoppel. She had not been mistaken about her rights in the home: on the contrary, she clearly knew that she was not entitled to a share because she had asked for her name to be included on the deeds and he had refused. Even if this conclusion was incorrect, she had not acted relying upon the mistaken belief: her acting as a wife and mother and her paying for decorating and central heating were not behaviour that indicated a reliance upon a mistaken belief as to her rights in the home.

Pascoe v. Turner (C.A. 1979)

After a relationship of several years had broken down, the man reassured the lady that the house and everything in it were hers. Subsequently, she paid for substantial improvements to the property. The court upheld her claim to a share in the home, even though it was in the sole name of the man, on the basis of proprietary estoppel.

Once it is established that the claimant should be allowed to assert a right to the home contrary to that of the legal owner, the question that must then be answered is the extent of her right. In *Pascoe* v. *Turner*, Cumming-Bruce L.J. asked of himself what was "the minimum equity to do justice to her, having regard to the way in which she changed her position for the worse" and decided that the only just solution was that she should be given the whole of the house. Obviously, the relief ordered in any other case will be totally dependent on the facts that have led to the claim.

OCCUPATION OF THE HOME

If a woman is successful in establishing that she has a beneficial interest in the property, she may then be faced with a demand that nevertheless the property be sold so that the man may at least realise his share. This could equally happen to a woman who is a joint owner on the face of the deeds. An immediate sale of the home, on the breakdown of the relationship, can cause just as much hardship to an unmarried woman as it can to a wife, even if she does receive a share of the proceeds of sale.

By the Law of Property Act, s. 30 the court can order the sale of property subject to a trust for sale (as most jointly owned property is). But it can also refuse to make such an order. Generally it will do so if satisfied that the purpose of the trust is still unfulfilled. Thus if the home was in reality bought as a home for the family, it is likely that any application for the sale of the home prior to any children reaching their majority will be refused, despite the fact that the relationship of the adults has broken down. Thus the woman's occupation is protected to a limited extent.

But because of the facts of their relationships, some women are not able to establish that they own a share of the property. As a last resort, such a woman may at least be able to establish a right to occupy the home after the relationship has broken down, even if she cannot establish a right to a share in the beneficial ownership.

This may be possible if the circumstances show that he has granted her a licence to remain on his property, a licence that was given for consideration and which cannot therefore be revoked by giving reasonable notice but only in accordance with the contract. By the very nature of things, once more the court will usually be asked to infer that such a licence was granted from the conduct of the parties. Further, as in trust cases, the court is asked to infer what interests the parties intended: this will mean that the court will be asked to infer the terms of the licence, in particular, how long it was intended to last.

In *Tanner* v. *Tanner* (C.A. 1975), because the woman gave up a protected tenancy to go and live with the man and their children at his house, the court inferred that he had granted to her a licence to occupy his property until the children left school. However, in *Coombes* v. *Smith* the court rejected the alternative claim of the plaintiff to a licence for the duration of her life. (It was not asked to determine whether the facts led to the inference that she had been granted a licence while the children were of school age because the man had conceded this.)

It will be appreciated that inferring a licence and its terms is an extremely artificial exercise. An example of an even more artificial exercise is to be found in *Ungurian* v. *Lesnoff* (H.C. 1989). In this case, the court found that there was a common intent that the woman should be permitted to live in property vested in the man's sole name for the rest of her life. On the facts, this intent was not merely that she should have a licence irrevocable for life but that the man should hold the property on trust for the woman for her life. The court thus invoked all the provisions of the Settled Land Act 1925.

4. FINANCIAL PROVISION FOR CHILDREN

THE CHILD SUPPORT ACT 1991

In July 1990 the then Prime Minister, Mrs. Thatcher, announced that the Government intended to set up a Child Support Agency ("The Agency") to trace absent parents and make them accept their financial responsibilities for their children. In the ensuing White Paper *Children Come First* (1990) (Cmnd. 1263) the Government identified problems with the existing child maintenance system. "Unnecessarily fragmented, uncertain in its results, slow and ineffective. It is based largely on discretion . . . The cumulative effect is uncertainty and inconsistent decisions about how much maintenance should be paid". It was felt that child maintenance awards were generally too low and that too many fathers escaped liability completely. The C.S.A. gave effect to the White Paper with little amendment and came into force on April 5, 1993. The Agency is responsible for all new cases, for cases where the claimant is on income support and family credit, and by April 1997, alphabetically, all cases will fall within the remit of the Agency.

The underlying principle of the C.S.A. is that whatever the changes in parents relationships, they cannot change their responsibilities for their children. The C.S.A. achieves its aims by providing a formula for payment of maintenance and by giving wide powers to the Child Support Officers to obtain information, supplemented by powers of enforcement and collection. These provisions have priority over any powers of the Courts.

The C.S.A. applies to a "qualifying child" defined by section 3(1) as a child where one or both of his parents is an "absent parent". This somewhat emotive expression means a parent who is not living in the same household with the child, whatever the contact arrangements may be. The person with whom one child has his home and who provides him with day to day care is called "a person with care". It should be noted that the C.S.A. applies only to natural or adoptive parents or persons treated as parents under the H.F.E.A. The absent parent is required to make periodical payments in accordance with complicated, rigid formulae, the detail of which are beyond the scope of this work. However, the basic principles may be summarised thus.

First, the C.S.A. lays down a *maintenance requirement* which is the amount needed to maintain the child based on income support criteria.

Second, the *maintenance assessment* is the assessable income of the absent parent, adding the income of the person with care and dividing by two.

Controversially, in assessing the absent parent's "assessable income", only reasonable housing costs (which may not be the full cost) may not be allowable and no account is taken of the cost of maintaining children living with him who are not children of the first marriage, *e.g.* step-children or children of a second union.

There is also an *additional element* whereby the absent parent can be called upon to pay further amounts up to a statutory maximum where the total assessable income exceeds the maintenance requirement.

Finally, the *protected income* level is designed to ensure that the absent parent should be better off than he would be on income support. The assessment is thus adjusted so that he keeps £8 per week plus 10 per cent. of the amount by which his income exceeds income support level.

Once the assessment is made, the Agency may carry out collection and enforcement and will automatically do so where the claimant is on income support.

The Agency may make deductions from earnings orders under section 31, may apply to the Magistrates for a liability order under section 33, and in the event of wilful refusal or culpable neglect, imprisonment for up to six weeks under section 40.

By virtue of section 9(1), no agreement for maintenance can prevent a person with care from applying for an assessment and any clause purporting to exclude that right is void. This provision has achieved public notoriety because of the effect it has had on parents who had made clean break agreements under the M.C.A. on the basis that the periodical payments to or for the children would be nominal. The C.S.A. retrospectively overrides such agreements in respect of the periodical payments but does not affect the capital element, which, in most cases, has been the transfer of the former matrimonial home. Section 9(1) also virtually ensures that no future agreements for a clean break can be made between couples with minor children, because the parent with care will always be able to apply for an assessment.

The maintenance assessment can only be made on application to the Agency, but in respect of persons with care on benefit, they must authorise action on penalty of a reduction in benefit under section 46(5) of 20 per cent. for 26 weeks, followed by 10 per cent. for a further year. Under section 6(2) and section 46(3) the requirement to co-operate may be waived if an officer is satisfied that there is a risk to the claimant or any child of suffering harm or undue distress.

Maintenance Assessments and Special Cases Regulations 1992 give relief to an absent parent who has regular contact with his child. The assessment is reduced if the child spends 104 nights or more per year with the absent parent. On the face of it, this is a reasonable provision but practitioners have reported an increase in contested contact cases. The person with care will want to keep contact below 104 nights so that there is no loss of maintenance, whilst the absent parent will seek just the opposite. Similar disputes may arise where a child spends time with both parents, 183 nights deciding whether the parent has care or is an absent parent.

C.S.A., s. 2 provides that "the welfare of the child shall be taken into account" but it makes no reference to it being a "first" (as in M.C.A.) or "paramount" (as in CA) consideration. Perhaps this is not surprising when one considers other sections of the C.S.A., particularly the reduced benefit direction (which can hardly be in the child's interest), the fact that the assessment reduces state benefits in the hands of the carer pound for pound and that children of second families are largely ignored. Little wonder, then, that many critics of the C.S.A. conclude that the C.S.A. benefits the Treasury more than it does the children. Additionally, arguments about the level of contact can only add to the bitterness and distress in the breakdown of relationships which the 1969 reforms and the 1994 proposals sought to eliminate.

Few would argue with the basic principle of the C.S.A. that parents are financially responsible for their children but the lack of flexibility in the calculation, the absence of appeals and its disregard for previous arrangements have caused exceptional hardship to some parents who have second families or those who have made clean break settlements prior to the introduction of the C.S.A. See *Crozier* v. *Crozier* (C.A. 1993).

Although the C.S.A. supplants the Court's powers, the sections of the M.C.A. and CA dealing with child maintenance are not repealed and it is still necessary to discuss these provisions. The Courts will have a role in any of the following circumstances.

(i) Where the absent parent is sufficiently wealthy to be able to "top up" the maximum maintenance which can be assessed under C.S.A.

(ii) Where the child is receiving full-time instruction or training requiring provision of some or all of the expenses, *e.g.* school fees.

(iii) Where the child is disabled, orders may be made to meet some or all of the expenses attributable to that disability.

(iv) Where 17 and 18 year olds are not in full-time education.

(v) Where there is to be a lump sum or transfer of property order.

(vi) Where the child is a "child of the family" and not a qualifying child.

Orders for Children under Matrimonial Causes Act 1973

Within the limitations of the above conditions children can have the same types of orders made in their favour, against either of the parties to the marriage as can the parties themselves.

The order can direct payment to the child or some third party for the child's benefit. Obviously, the "third party" will usually be the parent who has the child living with him.

Generally, no application for an order in favour of a child over 18 can be made. The orders can be made on the grant of a decree or at any time afterwards, but it should be noted that in the case of periodical payments, secured and unsecured, and lump sum the order can also be made before the grant of a decree or, if the proceedings for decree are unsuccessful, on the dismissal of the petition or within a reasonable time afterwards. Thus, to a certain extent, children can be provided for independently of a decree.

Periodical payments orders secured or unsecured must terminate when the child reaches 17, unless the court considers that the welfare of the child requires the order to extend beyond that age. Further, neither order can extend beyond 18 unless the court is satisfied that the child is still (or would be) receiving education or training for employment or there are other special circumstances. Finally, both types of periodical payments orders must cease on the death of the payer, even secured payments.

Matters Taken into Account when Making Orders

As with spouse orders, the first consideration of the court, when deciding whether and how to exercise its powers, is the welfare of any minor children of the family.

The courts are provided with a list of matters that they must have regard to by the M.C.A., s. 25(3):

(a) the financial needs of the child
(b) the income, earning capacity, property and other financial resources of the child
(c) any physical or mental disability of the child
(d) the type of education or training he was receiving or was expected to receive by the parties to the marriage
(e) the financial assets and needs of the parties, the standard of living enjoyed by the family prior to the breakdown of the marriage, and any physical or mental disability of the parties.

The M.C.A., s. 25(4) provides further factors to be taken into account when the Court is considering making an order against a party to the marriage who is not a parent of the child, and include, for example the liability of any other person to maintain the child.

Orders under Section 15 of The Children Act 1989

Section 15 of the CA provides for the grant of a range of financial and property awards for the benefit of a child subject to the C.S.A. The applicant must be the parent (or guardian) of the child and orders can be made against a parent.

It must be remembered that the availability of these orders is not dependent upon the parties being married to each other; it is dependent upon parenthood. However, married parents may make use of section 15 where there is no pending divorce proceedings.

Once parenthood has been established, the Court has the power to make the following orders:

(a) that either parent pay periodical payments for the benefit of the child, secured or unsecured
(b) that either parent pay a lump sum for the benefit of the child
(c) that either parent transfer property to which he is entitled to the child
(d) that either parent do settle such property for the benefit of the child.

Payments and transfer for the benefit of the child can be ordered to be made direct to the child himself or to some third party. (It should be noted that if the application is made to a magistrates' court, the only orders that can be made are ones for unsecured periodical payments and lump sum not exceeding £1,000.)

All the above orders benefit children alone. Subject to this limitation, the range of orders available under the CA, s. 15 is wide, almost equivalent to those available ancillary to decree proceedings.

Orders for unsecured periodical payments cease on the death of the payer and for both types of periodical payment the rules for cessation when the child reaches a specified age, covered in Chapter 2 in connection with the M.C.A., apply.

The CA Schedule 1 lists the matters that the court must take into account when deciding what order to make. They bear some similarity to those listed in the M.C.A., s. 25(3), the factors relevant for child orders ancillary to decree proceedings.

Perhaps the most important question concerning the CA, s. 15, is the extent to which the courts will be persuaded to exercise their powers to grant transfer and settlement orders in favour of a child. This is of particular importance to an unmarried mother who has her child living with her, as such an order against her former partner will indirectly benefit her, a result she might not otherwise achieve directly by use of the principles discussed in Chapter 3. On the basis of the decision in *H.* v. *M.* (*Property: Beneficial Interest*) (1992), the outlook is not promising.

5. DOMESTIC VIOLENCE

Violence in the family is not unknown. It can occur in many forms including behaviour which falls short of violence in the accepted sense of the word. It may cause the breakdown of a relationship or arise from it: the victim may not even accept that the relationship is ended.

It should be remembered that physical violence wherever and with whom committed is a criminal offence. In the landmark decision of *R.* v. *R.* (1992) the House of Lords ruled that a husband can rape his wife, overturning the medieval common law. However, the criminal law is primarily concerned with punishment and does not always adequately protect the victim. Therefore this chapter is concerned with civil remedies of which the most effective is the injunction. An injunction can be granted not only to restrain violence but also to restrain "molestation". For the sake of brevity, the term violence will be used in this chapter but will include, unless otherwise stated, molestation as well.

Horner v. *Horner* (CA 1983) defined molestation as "any conduct which can properly be regarded as such a degree of harassment as to call for the intervention of the Court". For example, injunctions were granted in the following cases:

Horner v. Horner

The husband hung scurrilous posters about his wife on the railings of the school where she worked.

Spencer v. Camacho (1983)

Inter alia, he searched through her handbag without her permission.

Johnson v. Walton (1990)

He sent nude photographs of his former lover to the newspapers.

There are cases where an injunction restraining such behaviour will not be sufficient protection. Families living under the same roof while a relationship is breaking down are subject to all sorts of pressures which cannot always be solved by non-molestation orders. Sometimes, they simply add to the pressures.

In these cases, there may be no real alternative but to make an order separating the parties, an order which ousts one of them from the home. Not surprisingly, they are called ouster orders but they can have many variations: for example, to prevent one party using certain rooms in the house, see *E.* v. *E.* (1994) or an ouster from the house and even the area in which it is situated.

It is most commonly the woman who seeks an order against the man and this assumption is used throughout the chapter. The powers can be equally used by a man against a woman. It should also be noted that orders can be granted for the protection of children in the family, under the powers granted by the CA, discussed in more detail in Chapters 7 and 8.

Perhaps most important of all, it should be remembered that the powers of the Court derive from a "hotchpot of legislation": different statutes give different courts their powers, often similar but really quite distinct. It is an unsatisfactory state of affairs but there is presently no alternative but to be aware of the sources of the powers and their differences.

THE INHERENT JURISDICTION

By section 37(1) of the S.C.A., the High Court is given the power to grant injunctions "in all cases in which it appears to the court to be just and convenient to do so." This power is also given to the county court by section 38 of the C.C.A. Both provisions re-enact earlier statutes and are sometimes referred to as "the inherent jurisdiction." This reflects the fact that the courts had developed the power to grant injunctions long before they were first given it by statute. The provisions are the source of the courts' powers to grant injunctions in all sorts of cases (not merely matrimonial causes), and of all types (not only those that are required for the protection of members of the family).

In the family law sphere, this power is frequently used to grant non-molestation injunctions as a part of a divorce suit. Obviously, if the wife requiring protection does not want a divorce then she will not choose to apply for the injunction under this power: there are others more suitable to her needs. But if she does, then the powers given to the courts under the S.C.A./C.C.A. provide a very convenient way of bringing all proceedings together. The language of section 37 would lead to the conclusion that the courts have a very wide power to grant both non-molestation and ouster injunctions, a power that is only limited by the phrase "just and convenient." In fact this is not so, for the courts have continued to impose on the use of the power, limitations that they developed when their powers were truly "inherent."

An injunction under these Acts can only be granted in support of a legal or equitable right. In many of the decided cases, the nature of the right that was being supported by the injunction granted is not explored. But in some, this has been the point at issue and it has been variously explained.

It is accepted that everyone has a right not to be subjected to assault and battery and this has often been relied on by the courts, either expressly or impliedly, when granting a wife a non-molestation injunction against her violent husband, as a part of divorce proceedings. It is possible, however, that such injunctions are too wide.

Patel v. *Patel* (C.A. 1988)

An injunction restraining the respondent from "assaulting, molesting or otherwise interfering or communicating with the applicant" had been granted to an unmarried woman as a part of an action alleging trespass to the person. It was redrawn by the court to restrain assault and molestation only. This was ordered on the basis that there is no right not to be harassed that could be supported by the words "otherwise interfering or communicating with . . ."

However, sometimes, the courts have declared that a wife, as a litigant, has the right not to be subjected to undue pressure to abandon divorce proceedings and have granted her a non-molestation injunction against her violent husband during the currency of the proceedings.

Ouster injunctions present a different problem. Since *Richards* v. *Richards*, applications for ouster orders between spouses have to be made under the M.H.A. In practice, they may still be dealt with as part of the divorce proceedings but the Court must apply the principles of the M.H.A. in arriving at their decision.

There have been conflicting decisions in the Court of Appeal concerning the power to grant ouster orders in proceedings concerning children.

In *Ashbury* v. *Millington* (1986) the Court said it had no powers under the Guardianship of Minors Act 1971, nor was there power under the inherent jurisdiction.

This decision has been confirmed as correct by:

Re F (Minors) (Parental Home: Ouster) (1993)

Mother argued that father should be excluded from the house so that she could live there with the children. She relied on the inherent jurisdiction and in the alternative, a CA, s. 8 specific issue order. Her appeal was dismissed. An injunction under the inherent jurisdiction was not available (confirming *Ashbury* v. *Millington*) and section 8 orders could not affect the father's right of occupation. It was suggested that there could have been jurisdiction under the CA, s. 15.

Finally, the injunction sought must bear a sensible relationship to the proceedings in which it is sought. It has long been accepted that non-molestation and ouster orders bear such a relationship to divorce proceedings because, as was stated in *McGibbon* v. *McGibbon* (H.C. 1973)

> "the court in dealing with such a cause is essentially concerned with enquiring into and regulating the personal relationship of the parties to each other".

However, a non-molestation order does not bear a sensible relationship to proceedings for maintenance *Des Salles d'Epinoix* v. *Des Salles d'Epinoix* (C.A. 1967) nor does an ouster injunction bear a sensible relationship to proceedings under the Inheritance (Provision for Family and Dependants) Act 1975.

The Principle in *Richards* v. *Richards* (H.L. 1983)

There is an important limitation on the apparently very wide powers of the court under the S.C.A., s. 37(1). In the case of *Richards* v. *Richards* the court decided that the power could not be used to regulate the occupation of the matrimonial home because Parliament had enacted a statute specifically designed to cover this problem, the Matrimonial Homes Act 1967 (now 1983). It was not open to litigants to avoid the detailed provisions of an Act designed to meet a specific problem by calling in aid an earlier and more general power. Many ouster orders (which in effect regulate the occupation of the matrimonial home) had been made under the general power contained in the S.C.A., s. 37(1), between the operational date of the Matrimonial Homes Act 1967 and the delivery of the judgments in *Richards* v. *Richards* and their jurisdictional basis was thus undermined.

It therefore becomes necessary to consider the provisions of the M.H.A., to see exactly what orders can be made under that jurisdiction, for if an applicant requires an order within the powers of the court under the M.H.A., then that Act must be used. Equally, it is arguable that if an applicant requires an order that cannot be granted under the M.H.A., then the general power to grant ouster injunctions can still be invoked.

THE MATRIMONIAL HOMES ACT 1983

Where at least one spouse has a right of occupation in a dwelling that at one time has been the matrimonial home the court has the power, on the application of either spouse, *inter alia*, to make an order

    (a) restricting or terminating those rights
    (b) prohibiting, suspending or restricting the exercise of those rights
    (c) requiring either spouse to permit the exercise by the other of those rights.

A right of occupation can be created in many ways. One or both of the parties may own the property and of course ownership gives a right of occupation. Such a right can also be created by contract, for example a tenancy or licence. Finally, as has been discussed in Chapter 2, a spouse may have the statutory rights of occupation themselves created by the M.H.A. These rights too are capable of being affected by order under the M.H.A.

It will be appreciated that when a court makes an order, for example, terminating a husband's right of occupation (however derived), in effect, if not in form, he has been ousted. The power to restrict rights of occupation could be used to apportion the house between the spouses and, in effect, to create an ouster of part.

The powers of the court under the M.H.A. do, however, have limitations. First, it would not seem to be possible to oust a spouse from an area around the matrimonial home. Arguably therefore, in principle, such an order may still be made under the general power to grant injunctions, which was often so used prior to the case of *Richards* v. *Richards*. Secondly, there is no power to grant non-molestation injunctions under the M.H.A. Thirdly, the M.H.A. applies only to married partners.

An application under the M.H.A. is a separate set of proceedings in its own right. This, therefore, is a way to obtain an order regulating the occupation of the matrimonial home without at the same time issuing any other matrimonial proceedings, such as divorce, a result that may be desired by some spouses. However, if the applicant does also want, for example, a divorce, then, by special provision of the rules of court, M.H.A. proceedings can and should be issued ancillary to those proceedings.

THE EXERCISE OF THE COURT'S POWERS

The M.H.A. spells out the principles to be applied in the grant of ouster injunctions. By section 1(3) of the M.H.A., the court may make such order regulating the occupation of the matrimonial home "as it thinks just and reasonable having regard to:

(a) the conduct of the spouses in relation to each other
(b) their respective needs and financial resources
(c) the needs of any children
(d) all the circumstances of the case."

Conduct of the Parties
Conduct of all types can be taken into account by the court, but obviously, the more serious it is, the more likely it is to have an effect on the success of the application. Violence and threats of violence are relevant but such lesser types of behaviour as quarrelling, aggression and abuse will sometimes count too, as will behaviour that has an effect on the spouse though not specifically directed at her, *e.g.* frequent drunkenness. If, as a part of an application for an ouster order the wife complains of the husband's conduct and states that she cannot live with him because of it, the court must assess whether or not the wife has reasonable grounds for her refusal to live with the husband. If the court reaches the conclusion that she has not, this does not automatically prevent the court from making an order in her favour—there are, after all a number of other factors for the court to consider—but as stated in *Richards* v. *Richards*:

> "in a substantial number of cases at any rate it will be a factor of such weight as to lead a court to think that it would not be just or reasonable to allow her application."

Needs and Resources of the Parties
The parties' income, capital assets, living expenses and debts will all be relevant under this head. Perhaps not so obvious, but a factor that has continually been stressed by the court as being of great relevance, is the accommodation needs of the parties. The court will consider what would happen to each of the parties in the event of granting or refusing the ouster application, and, if there are children, will also bear in mind that one of the parties, usually the wife, has to have accommodation not only for herself but also for the children. Thus, the result of not making an order

ousting the husband, in a case where the wife reasonably refuses to live with him, will be that the wife, and often the children, will be forced to leave the home, if they have not done so already. What accommodation prospects does she have? Can she rent or buy and does she have the income resources for this? Will she be forced to rely, at least for some time, on the generosity of friends or relatives or the local availability of a woman's refuge, accommodation that will often be cramped? However, the court cannot totally ignore the husband's needs for accommodation if he is ousted, albeit that he only needs housing for himself, so many of the same questions will be asked, and the courts have recognised that today it is often difficult for even a single person to obtain accommodation.

Needs of the Children

If the children are being abused directly, then their need for protection is obviously a factor of great importance. As has already been mentioned, the court will also take into account the needs of the children for accommodation. However, the needs of the children are recognised as extending further than their physical and material wants and the court accepts that their emotional needs must also be taken into account. For example, it is accepted that, ideally, children need a stable environment, free from the tensions and anxiety created by the sight of parents quarrelling or fighting, and preferably in a home that they are used to, the matrimonial home.

The Balance between the Factors

In *Richards* v. *Richards*, it was decided that none of the factors listed in the M.H.A., s. 1(3), including the needs of the children, was to be accorded a priority or paramountcy over the others. This is in striking contrast to the principle contained in the CA, s. 1(1), which states that "when a court decides any question with respect to the upbringing of a child . . . the child's welfare shall be the court's paramount consideration." In effect therefore, *Richards* v. *Richards* decided that ouster applications do not involve the courts in decisions concerning the upbringing of children. It is the case that *Richards* v. *Richards* was decided a number of years before the CA came into force, but it was decided taking into account a very similar principle contained in the Guardianship of Minors Act 1971 (now repealed). It is therefore suggested that *Richards* v. *Richards* is still good law and that ouster applications are not subject to the CA, s. 1(1).

However, it was accepted in *Richards* v. *Richards* that, in any given case, the needs of the children may be so claimant that the court, in exercising its discretion under the M.H.A., s. 1(3), could correctly give paramountcy to them. A striking example of such a case is that of

T. v. *T.* (C.A. 1987) (unreported)

> The parties and their four children, aged between three and 16, were all living together at the matrimonial home. After earlier proceedings that resulted in a non-molestation injunction in favour of the wife, there had been no violence between the parties. Nevertheless, the atmosphere at the home was extremely tense and the parties were frequently quarrelling. As a result, the children were showing marked psychological effects, including bedwetting and soiling. Further, a local authority social worker gave evidence that the authority were so concerned about the development of the children that they were seriously considering applying for a care order, believing that there was no prospect of helping the children while they remained in the home with both parents. The court at first instance found that the situation was the fault of both parents, that it would therefore be unfair to the husband to oust him and refused to do so. The Court of Appeal reversed that decision, clearly giving the children's needs a priority.

However it is suggested that such a decision should be treated with caution and that it will be appreciated, from what is discussed below, that it depended upon its own very exceptional facts.

Such Order as is "Just and Reasonable"

Apart from the factors specifically mentioned in the M.H.A., s. 1(3) the court is enjoined to make such order as is "just and reasonable." In a number of recent cases, the Court of Appeal has reminded lower courts that they must also take into account the Draconian nature of an ouster order. As was stated in *Wiseman* v. *Simpson* (C.A. 1988):

> "To order any man or woman to leave his or her home is a drastic thing to do. The importance of a home is to be measured not only by the strength of the tie created by time to one particular place but also by the difficulty in getting another."

With a number of factors to be considered by the court, it would seem that it has a balancing exercise to do, that it has to consider all of the factors in favour of the wife's case and compare them with the factors that support the husband's case. It would not be illogical to suppose that the party who is found to have the stronger case at the end of this exercise should succeed. Certainly, the court does have a balancing exercise to complete, but having done this, again as was stated in *Wiseman* v. *Simpson*:

> "It can only be just and reasonable to make an ouster order if the case of the party claiming the order is not only stronger on those matters than the other party's case but is such as to justify making an order that a man or woman be ousted from his or her home."

The facts of *Wiseman* v. *Simpson* are instructive for they bear a certain similarity to the facts of *T.* v. *T.* yet no ouster order was granted by the Court of Appeal.

Wiseman v. *Simpson*

> There was no recent history of violence between the parties but there was a very tense atmosphere in the home caused by their frequent quarrels. The man had refused to give the woman any housekeeping and she had refused to perform any housekeeping duties. Eventually she had locked him out. In resisting his application for re-entry, the woman alleged that the situation was retarding the development of their 18-month-old child. Evidence was also given that the only other accommodation available to her was sharing a room in her parents' house and that, if both she and her partner remained in the home, she could not claim state benefits for her support.

> In rescinding the grant of the first instance ouster order and remitting the case back to the county court for a rehearing, the Court of Appeal stated that, although the judge had taken into account all of the factors listed in the M.H.A., s. 1(3), the drastic nature of the ouster order had not been considered. Further, the court clearly felt that the evidence of damage to the child was very weak.

THE DOMESTIC VIOLENCE AND MATRIMONIAL PROCEEDINGS ACT 1976

By section 1 of the D.V.A. a spouse may apply for one or more of the four types of injunctions, *i.e.*:

(a) a non-molestation injunction relating to the applicant
(b) a non-molestation injunction relating to any child living with the applicant
(c) an ouster injunction, relating to the matrimonial home, a part of it or an area around it
(d) an injunction requiring the other spouse to permit the applicant to enter and remain in the home or a part of it.

Although the Act puts no limit on the duration of any orders granted under in, it is seen as an emergency measure and, in practice, the court will consider putting time limits on most ouster injunctions. Three months has been suggested as appropriate.

An application under the D.V.A. is a separate set of proceedings in its own right. Again, therefore, such an application provides a way to obtain an order for protection without at the same time having to issue, for example, divorce proceedings. Under this jurisdiction, however, non-molestation injunctions as well as ouster injunctions are available, a wider form of protection than that given by the M.H.A. alone. The Act is often used by spouses who do not want or cannot obtain a divorce.

By section 1(2) of the D.V.A., the powers of the court to grant injunctions under section 1(1) apply also to "a man and a woman who are living with each other in the same household as husband and wife" (referred to afterwards as "cohabitees").

The extension of the court's powers under the D.V.A. to co-habitees has not been without its problems. Almost immediately, there was an attempt to limit the grant of injunctions to cases where there was a legal right that needed the protection of the injunction (by analogy with the general power). Had this argument been successful, this would have been disastrous for many cohab-itees requiring ouster injunctions. Cohabitees do not have a right to occupy the home as a result of their status. Thus, only those with a right (and possibly the sole right) to occupy the home either by property or contract law would have been able to obtain an ouster. Fortunately, in *Davis* v. *Johnson* (H.L. 1978) the Lords rejected this argument.

Davis v. *Johnson* also highlighted another problem of interpreta-tion in the D.V.A., which again could have led to large numbers of cohabitees being excluded from the scope of the Act. Section 1(2) permits a man and a woman who "are" living with each other to make an application for an injunction, yet many cohabitees who are treated with violence flee the home and then make an applica-tion from temporary and often very inadequate accommodation. The Court of Appeal stated *obiter* that the fact that the parties were not living together at the time of application should not bar the application, if they had been living together at the time of the incidents giving rise to the application.

This sympathetic and sensible interpretation, which has been followed in a number of cases since, gives rise to a further problem wever. Is there any stage after the separation that the court s the jurisdiction to grant relief under the D.V.A.? In *O'Neill*

v. *Williams* (C.A. 1984) it was stated that the court always has the jurisdiction, if the above test is satisfied, but "the longer the time that elapses the less and less likely it will become that any judge would exercise it."

The phrase "a man and woman living with each other in the same household as husband and wife" is not defined. It is similar to the phrase "living with each other in the same household" contained in M.C.A., s. 2(6), and it is tempting to assume that the same test should be applied under the D.V.A. as is under the M.C.A. whenever this point is in issue (see Chapter 1). It must be borne in mind, however, that the decision on such an issue has very different results in the two jurisdictions. If the parties are found not to be living together, then the court has no jurisdiction to grant relief under the D.V.A.; whereas, under the M.C.A., such a decision would mean the grant of relief in the shape of a decree. It is possible that this distinction explains the somewhat unusual case of

Adeoso v. *Adeoso* (C.A. 1980)

> The unmarried applicant for an injunction under the D.V.A. was still living under the same roof as her partner but there was very little contact between them. She slept in one room, he in another. She did not cook or wash for him. They did not speak, communicating by notes. However, their home was only a two roomed flat.
>
> **Held**: it was impossible to describe the parties as "living apart," despite the fact that such arrangements would, on earlier case law, have constituted "separate households." The court deprecated the strained interpretation of the law had been developed in the earlier cases and refused to adopt it. An injunction was granted.

An application under the D.V.A. is far less cumbersome than an application for an injunction as a part of a tort action. However, the D.V.A. only applies to men and women who are living with each other, albeit this phrase is sympathetically interpreted. There are those who need protection, but who have either never lived together or who parted too long ago for the court to accept jurisdiction under the D.V.A. Such persons are outside the ambit of the D.V.A. and will still need to use the cumbersome procedure of an application for an injunction within a tort action.

THE EXERCISE OF THE COURT'S POWERS

Before it will grant a non-molestation injunction, the court must be satisfied that there has been some form of molestation, as defined earlier in this chapter, and also that there is a need for an order preventing a repetition of the behaviour. Obviously, the type of the behaviour, and the likelihood of its happening again will be relevant.

Applications for ouster orders can also be made under the D.V.A., a statute which does not specify the principles upon which the court should act in granting orders under it. *Obiter dicta* in the judgments of *Richards* v. *Richards* at least imply that the factors mentioned in the M.H.A., s. 1(3), should be taken into account on applications under the D.V.A. too and this has been confirmed by a number of cases: for example, *Wiseman* v. *Simpson*. It has even been decided that the factors listed in the M.H.A., s. 1(3), are relevant to an application under the D.V.A. by a cohabitee (*Lee* v. *Lee* (C.A. 1984)). This decision is particularly surprising when it is remembered that the M.H.A. is a statute that applies only to married partners.

THE DOMESTIC PROCEEDINGS AND MAGISTRATES' COURTS ACT 1978

By section 16 of the D.P.M.C.A. a spouse may apply to a magistrates' court for either or both of two types of orders:

(a) an order that the other spouse should not use or threaten to use violence against the applicant or a child of the family (a personal protection order)
(b) an order that the other spouse should leave and/or not enter the matrimonial home (an exclusion order) and, if appropriate, should permit the applicant to enter and remain in the matrimonial home.

It should be stressed that, in this jurisdiction, the word "violence" means just that: the magistrates' court has no power to restrain molestation that does not involve violence or a threat of it.

Further, it should also be noted that the magistrates' court has no power to grant relief to an unmarried partner. Nor does it have the power to exclude from an area around the home.

To obtain an order forbidding the use of threats of violence the applicant must prove the use or threat of violence by the respondent against either the applicant or a child of the family and that the order is necessary for the protection of either of them.

To obtain the order excluding the respondent from the home, applicant must prove that she or a child of the family is in ʒer of physical injury and one of the following three conditions:

(a) the use of violence by the respondent against the applicant or a child of the family

(b) the use of violence by the respondent against some third person and the threat of violence against the applicant or a child of the family

(c) the threat of violence by the respondent against the applicant or a child of the family in breach of an order forbidding the same.

It will be noted that, as is to be expected, the conditions that must be proved before an order excluding the respondent from the home will be made are far more stringent than those relating to an order simply forbidding the use or threat of violence.

ENFORCEMENT

It is one thing to obtain an injunction or order designed to protect family members and quite another to ensure that it is obeyed. In many cases, such orders are broken and the topic of how to enforce obedience to such orders is, in practice, very important.

It is obvious that no court can directly force respondents to comply with such orders. Applicants must rely on the court's powers to punish respondents for disobedience and hope that this (or the threat of it) will, indirectly, force respondents to obey such orders in the future. Breach of an injunction granted by either the High Court or the county court is contempt and is punishable by either a fine or, more usually in this context, imprisonment. Strictly, breach of an order made by the magistrates' court is not contempt. Nevertheless, by section 63 of the Magistrates' Court Act 1980, the magistrates' court also has the power to fine or imprison for breach of some orders, including those granted under the D.P.M.C.A., s. 16.

To obtain the punishment of the respondent by either of these methods, the applicant must take the responsibility for the institution and continuation of the process, a factor that can cause great stress and anxiety for a person who has already undergone much. She will often seek the help of her solicitor at all stages of the process, thus increasing the costs, and the process takes time. To avoid some, if not all of these disadvantages, a power of arrest can be attached to injunctions and orders (the D.V.A., s. 2 and the D.P.M.C.A., s. 18). The effect of this, is that a police constable can arrest, without warrant, any person whom he reasonably suspects of having broken the order. The only initiative the appli-

cant must take is to contact the police immediately upon breach—
far better than having to wait until her solicitor's office and the
court office open—and they can take him into custody immediately. The police must bring such a person before the relevant
court within 24 hours, and the court can then punish by fine or
imprisonment.

The exercise of a power of arrest has immediate and dire
consequences for the alleged offender. Consequently, its grant is
hedged about by limitations in both jurisdictions.

Under the D.V.A., the court must be satisfied that the respondent has caused actual bodily harm to the applicant or a child
living with her and is likely to do so again. The phrase "actual
bodily harm" has recently been interpreted by the courts in
Kendrick v. *Kendrick* (C.A. 1990): physical injury is not necessary,
if there is clear evidence of real psychological damage. Further,
a power of arrest can only be attached to injunctions restraining
the use of violence against the applicant or a child living with
her (and the word violence is used in section 2 in contrast to the
use of the word molestation in section 1) or to injunctions excluding the respondent from the matrimonial home.

However, the power to attach a power of arrest to an injunction
is not limited to injunctions granted under the D.V.A. itself: it is
available "when, on the application of a spouse, a court grants
an injunction" of the relevant type. Thus, a power of arrest has
also been attached to such injunctions granted under the general
power in the S.C.A., s. 37.

It should be noted, however, that there is doubt in some quarters
as to whether an order granted under the M.H.A. is an injunction
at all and therefore covered by the D.V.A., s. 2. Further, on the
wording of section 2, the application for an injunction must have
been made by a spouse. For the purposes of section 2, the word
"spouse" again includes cohabitees, but this is as has been interpreted by the courts (see above). Thus, an unmarried woman
who cannot use the D.V.A. to obtain an injunction, cannot use
the D.V.A. to obtain a power of arrest to any injunction that has
been granted to her within a tort action.

Orders granted under the D.P.M.C.A. are not covered by the
D.V.A., s. 2, but by the D.P.M.C.A., s. 18. Again, however, only
some of the orders that can be granted under the D.P.M.C.A.,
s. 16, can have a power of arrest attached to them; those forbidding
e use of violence against the applicant or a child of the family
the respondent and those forbidding the entry of the home by
respondent. Again, the court must be satisfied that stringent

conditions exist before it can attach a power of arrest; that the applicant or a child of the family has been physically injured by the respondent and that it is likely to happen again.

PROPOSALS FOR THE FUTURE

In 1984 Lord Scarman was critical of "the hotchpot of enactments" which covered this issue, and so was the Law Commission in its report on Domestic Violence and Occupation of the family home (No. 207, 1992). The Commission made some radical proposals. With regard to non-molestation orders, it proposed that all courts be given power to make an order whenever it is just and reasonable to do so, having regard to all the circumstances including the need to secure the health, safety and well-being of the applicant or any relevant child. They recommended the power should be extended to anyone associated with the respondent by virtue of a family or similar relationship, in particular, spouses and former spouses, co-habitants and former co-habitants, others living in the same household (other than tenants, lodgers, etc.), engaged and former engaged couples, parents and others with parental responsibility. Para 3.24 mentions also persons who have a sexual relationship (not necessarily involving intercourse) and cites as an example boy friend and girl friend in a romantic relationship. It clearly, and controversially, would include gay relationships as well.

The Commission also proposed the introduction of "Occupation Orders" available to anyone who is entitled to occupation of the home by virtue of a beneficial interest, contract or statutory right.

The right to occupation should extend against the same category of persons as the non-molestation order noted above.

The Court would be given the same powers as it has under M.H.A. All courts would have these powers, though the Magistrates would have to transfer cases to the County or High Court where determination of the right to occupy is a contested issue.

The Commission also proposed a strengthening of powers of arrest, including an obligatory attachment where there has been violence. Perhaps most controversially, it proposed that the police may apply for a civil remedy on behalf of a victim whether or not she consented to the proceedings. This was proposed to protect the intimidated and frightened victim who would not take such proceedings herself and help the police prevent further intimidation. The objections to allowing one person to take proceedings for another, against their will, seem self evident.

In the summer of 1994, in reply to a Parliamentary question, the Lord Chancellor said the Government intends to implement most of the recommendations "when a suitable opportunity occurs".

The proposal for the police to be able to pursue a civil remedy would not be implemented and the Government do not accept the inclusion of engaged couples, nor those who are in a sexual relationship not involving intercourse.

---

6. THE RELATIONSHIP BETWEEN CHILDREN AND ADULTS

All references to section numbers within this chapter are references to sections in the CA, unless otherwise stated.

At birth, the law defines a relationship between a child and his parents and no other adults. For many children, the law plays no further part in their upbringing, but, for some, events subsequent to their birth result in the need for additional principles. Parents may disagree about the child's upbringing; other adults may be the most appropriate carers. This chapter, therefore, covers the relationship between children and adults, not necessarily their parents, and also the principles the courts use when required to intervene and in some sense redraw the relationship created at birth.

The starting point is, however, the relationship between a child and his parents. Occasionally, the issue of exactly who is a parent arises.

Medical advances in human assisted reproduction have caused problems which resulted in the passing of H.F.E.A., which took effect on August 1, 1991 but relates only to births after that date. There are various types of assisted reproduction, including artifi-
ination, in vitro fertilisation (in lay terms, "test-tube"
t as either the sperm or the embryo (or both) may be
strangers, it means that a child may not be genetically
s "parents". The H.F.E.A., s. 27(1) provides "where
oman is carrying or has carried a child as a result

of placing in her an embryo, sperm or eggs ... [she] is the mother of the child".

As far as the male is concerned, the rule is that the genetic father (*i.e.* the donor of the sperm) is the legal father. However, there are two important exceptions to this rule. First, by section 28(2) "Where a married woman is carrying a child ... notwithstanding that the sperm was not donated by the husband, he and no other person is treated as the father of the child". This section will only apply if the husband consented to the wife's treatment. Second, by section 28(3), if donated sperm is used in the course of "licensed treatment" (*i.e.* licensed under H.F.E.A.) provided for a woman and a man together, then that man is treated as the father of the child. This section clearly covers the male co-habitant of the woman but is capable of even wider interpretation.

The H.F.E.A. also deals with surrogacy, where another woman (the surrogate mother) carries the child for a married couple following fertilisation using the gametes of one or both of the spouses. It should be noted that the Act does *not* apply where the surrogate is impregnated by sexual intercourse with the husband. Under section 30, the Court is empowered to make an order that the child is to be treated as a child of the parties to the marriage, but the following conditions *must* be satisfied:

1. the parties must be married to each other and be over 18 years of age
2. the order must be within six months of the birth
3. the court must be satisfied that the surrogate mother and the genetic father fully understand *and* consent to the order
4. the court must also be satisfied that no money changed hands in connection with the arrangements (commercial surrogacy is a criminal offence) but reasonable expenses, *e.g.* maternity clothes, travel, *etc* are allowed.

PATERNITY DISPUTES

Motherhood is rarely an issue; fatherhood often is, and whenever it falls to be considered, unless paternity is admitted, it must be proved.

Such an issue could arise within a number of different types of proceedings and the courts will often need to determine the paternity of the child as a preliminary matter. For example, only a father is entitled to apply for an order under CA, s. 4 (see later). If a man makes such an application, the mother may first deny that the child is his. If she were correct, then the court wc not have jurisdiction to grant the order sought. Therefore, faced with such a case, the court would first have to determine whether or not the child was the applicant's.

The question of paternity can also be dealt with as an issue in its own right. Under the Family Law Act 1986, a person can apply to the court simply for a declaration that a named person is his father.

Paternity disputes can arise between spouses but they more frequently arise between unmarried partners, possibly due to the following evidentiary point. Any children born to a married woman are presumed to be those of her husband. This presumption is rebuttable but this is not an easy task. There is no similar presumption to come to the aid of the unmarried man or woman who is asserting paternity, even if their relationship is stable and longstanding

Paternity can be established in a number of different ways: for example, evidence may be adduced of out of court admissions made by the man; of the fact that the man is registered as the father in the Register of Births Deaths and Marriages; of the man having had sexual intercourse with the mother at the time that conception must have taken place. None of these are conclusive and may or may not be accepted in any given case.

Conclusions drawn from the results of blood tests have also frequently been given as evidence in paternity cases. Until recently, the method of testing could not provide conclusive proof of paternity, but the advent of "D.N.A. fingerprinting" has dramatically altered the position. This can be used on any type of human tissue, for example, blood, hair, skin and semen, and can provide virtually conclusive proof of paternity. Despite the cost of the tests and the limited testing facilities, evidence gained by testing blood by D.N.A. fingerprinting is being used in paternity disputes more frequently.

D.N.A. fingerprinting is only of use if all parties, the mother, the child and the alleged father are tested. The Family Law Reform Act 1969 provides that, where the parentage of any person is in issue, the court may order that person or a party to the proceedings submit to blood tests. An amendment to the Act effected by the F.L.R.A. gives the court power to order the taking of any bodily samples. If anyone refuses to comply with the order, then the court may draw such inferences from this refusal as it

CHILDREN

ect of the physical relationship between parent and
times dependent upon whether the child was born

to married or unmarried parents. The phrase "a child whose mother and father were married at the time of his birth" is defined in the F.L.R.A., s. 1 and does include various children who were not literally born to parents who were married at the time of their births, for example, those who are legitimated by the subsequent marriage of their parents. In this book, the phrase "a child born to married parents" includes all those who are covered by the definition in the F.L.R.A., s. 1 and the phrase "a child born to unmarried parents" includes all those who are not.

At common law, a child born to unmarried parents had no rights against his father and remoter ancestors and, to begin with, no rights even against his mother: similarly, the adults had no duties towards him. Such a child often also felt a social stigma. Gradually, with changes in the law and society, the former and, it is hoped the latter, disadvantages were eroded if not entirely eradicated. Amendments in the legal position of the child born to unmarried parents have been effected by either extending the categories of children who were to be taken as having been born to married parents or by specifically providing that those born to unmarried parents should have some of the same rights as those born to married parents. Nevertheless, prior to the F.L.R.A., there still existed some significant differences in the legal positions of the two categories of children. The Act was designed to eradicate those differences as much as was thought reasonable. It was also designed to discourage the practice of labelling children either "legitimate" or "illegitimate."

First, the F.L.R.A. provides that, in the Act itself and in all subsequent legislation and instruments, wherever a relationship between two persons is referred to, in whatever way, it is to be interpreted without regard to the question of whether the parents or ancestors of one or both of them were married. This interpretation can be ousted by showing a contrary intent. Thus, whenever the word "child" appears in a statute or instrument enacted or entered into after the operational date of the F.L.R.A., this expression will be taken to mean every child, whether or not born to married parents unless otherwise stated. The new rule of construction has, therefore, reversed the trends of the past: no more will children born to unmarried parents expressly have to be included in a provision; if it is considered necessary to draw a distinction between the two categories of children, then the draftsman will have to expressly exclude one of them.

Secondly, the F.L.R.A. provides that the new rule of construction shall apply to certain statutes already on the statute prior to the F.L.R.A. In this way, the Act attempted to eradicate some of the legal differences that still existed between the two categories of children. For example, the F.L.R.A., s. 18 applies the new rule of construction to Part IV of the Administration of Estates Act 1925 and as a result the rights of children born to unmarried parents, to share in the distribution of an intestate's estate, are totally equated with the rights of children born to married parents.

The Law Commission, in its Report on Illegitimacy No. 157 stated that the new rule of construction would make it unnecessary to use adjectives (*i.e.* "legitimate" and "illegitimate") to label children and thereby hoped that the social and psychological effects of distinguishing between the two categories of children would be diminished. However, as a matter of policy, the F.L.R.A. does not eradicate all the legal differences between the two categories of children, and therefore does not eradicate the need to distinguish between them either. The Act does imply, however, that when in the future it is thought necessary to make the distinction, it should be made by referring to them as described at the beginning of this section.

One of the remaining distinctions drawn by the law between the two categories of children concerns the vesting of parental responsibility in their parents (see below).

PARENTAL RESPONSIBILITY

What is Parental Responsibility?

This concept is the legal definition of the relationship between parent and child (although sometimes, as will be seen, it also defines the relationship between other adults and a child). It is a new concept introduced by the CA. An appreciation of its nature, as discussed in the whole of this section, is of vital importance: the law relating to the resolution of disputes between private individuals (see Chapter 6) and the law relating to the protection of children by local authority intervention (see Chapter 7) are built upon it. During the passage through Parliament of th‸ ‸ ʰ Bill, the concept of parental responsibility was aptly ʰ the Lord Chancellor as

ʰread, knotting together parental status and the effect of the child's upbringing, whether in private family proceed- e proceedings . . .''

Previously, the parent/child relationship was thought, very loosely, to be one of parental rights, but in the last few decades this interpretation was criticised and gradually redefined. For example, Lord Scarman, in *Gillick* v. *West Norfolk Area Health Authority* and D.H.S.S. (H.L. 1985) stated that:

> "Parental rights are derived from parental duty and exist only so long as they are needed for the protection of the person and property of the child."

This view of parental duty being the key to the definition of the relationship between parent and child has received statutory acknowledgement in the CA.

Parental responsibility is defined by section 3 as

> "all the rights, duties, powers, responsibilities and authority which by law a parent of a child has in relation to the child and his property."

As will be appreciated, this definition is very general and does not list the sort of issues that are the subject of parental responsibility. Drawing upon cases prior to the CA, it is suggested that the concept includes the responsibility

(a) to have possession of the child and to take, on his behalf, all the many and minor decisions that arise every day
(b) to maintain contact with the child (obviously, only applicable if the child does not live with the parent)
(c) to actively consider and provide for the child's education
(d) to actively consider the need and provide for medical treatment on the child's behalf
(e) to administer the child's property
(f) to actively consider the wisdom of and consent or otherwise to the child's marriage between the ages of 16 and 18
(g) to protect the child from physical and moral danger
(h) to maintain the child financially.

To Whom does Parental Responsibility Belong?

At the birth of a child, the position is as follows: the parental responsibility for a child born to married parents belongs to both parents (s. 2(1)); the parental responsibility for a child born to unmarried parents belongs exclusively to the mother (s. 2(2)).

The Law Commission, in its Review of Child Law, Guardian-ship and Custody No. 172, recommended against the automatic creation of equal responsibility for unmarried parents. It was recognised that, while some children are born within stable unions, others are born as a result of a very casual relationship and it was not thought appropriate to give automatic parental responsibility to a man who, in practice, may have nothing to do with the child.

However, the Law Commission did feel that some provision for a sharing of parental responsibility between unmarried parents should be made. Accordingly, section 4 provides two methods whereby parental responsibility can be given to the unmarried father and thereafter shared with the mother.

First, it is possible for the parents to agree to share parental responsibility. The agreement, "a Parental Responsibility Agreement" must be in writing, in a prescribed form and recorded in the Principal Registry of the Family Division. In the alternative, the father may apply to the court, who can order that he shall share the parental responsibility for the child with the mother. Such an agreement or order is not permanent: either can be revoked by court order.

Parental responsibility, or a large part of it, can also be obtained by persons other than the parents of a child. There are several possibilities. For example, a parent with parental responsibility may, in writing, appoint a guardian for his child and such an appointment vests parental responsibility in the guardian (s. 5). Further, there are a number of court orders which, *inter alia*, have the effect of vesting parental responsibility in the person awarded the order, *e.g.* a residence order (see Chapter 6), an adoption order and a care order (see Chapter 7).

The Termination of Parental Responsibility

Apart from the appointment of a guardian or an agreement between unmarried parents, it is impossible for a person with parental responsibility to voluntarily surrender or transfer the whole or any part of it to another (s. 2(9)). The exercise of it may be delegated to a third party however.

Parental responsibility is not lost as a result of some other person subsequently acquiring it (s. 2(6)).

Subject to what is said below, parental responsibility can only be terminated by court order and only where this is specifically provided for.

For parents married when their child was born and an unmarried mother, parental responsibility can only be terminated by the grant of an adoption order in favour of someone else. Adoption also has this effect on others who have acquired parental responsibility. Further, their parental responsibility can be terminated by an order revoking or discharging the instrument, agreement or order that gave them parental responsibility.

Parental responsibility is owed to a child, defined in the CA as a person under the age of 18 (save for certain aspects of financial responsibility). Thus, generally, parental responsibility terminates automatically when the child reaches 18.

There is also a possibility that parental responsibility terminates automatically at some earlier though as yet ill defined point, as a result of the decision in *Gillick* v. *West Norfolk Area Health Authority & Another*. It must be emphasised that this is a case that predates the CA, as the following discussion of it, with its use of the term "parental rights," makes clear.

Gillick v. West Norfolk Area Health Authority & Another

The A.H.A. had issued to the doctors practising in its area a directive which contained guidelines as to when, in the view of the A.H.A., it would be lawful for a doctor to give contraceptive advice and treatment to a child under the age of 16, without the consent or even knowledge of the child's parent. The plaintiff sought a declaration that the directive was unlawful and one of her arguments was that such advice or treatment was an infringement of parental rights.

The majority of the Lords did not think that this was inevitably so. Lord Scarman stated, *inter alia*, that "parental rights yield to the right of the child to make his own decision when he reaches a sufficient understanding and intelligence to be capable of making up his own mind on the matter." Lord Bridge of Harwich agreed. Lord Fraser found no provision preventing him from holding that a girl under 16 lacked the legal capacity to consent to contraceptive advice and treatment provided "she has sufficient understanding and intelligence to know what they involve." Even Lord Templeman, who dissented, agreed that it was possible for a child to have capacity to consent to medical (but not contraceptive) treatment under the age of 16.

The case concerned the (then) parental right to consent to medical treatment, more specifically contraceptive treatment, but it is clear from the comments of various members of the Court quoted above that they were wide enough to cover all (then) parental rights. Thus it was arguable that all parental rights ceased as and when the child had the capacity to make the decision himself. In the light of the CA shifting the emphasis from rights to responsibilities, there is an argument that parental responsibility terminates when the child has the capacity to make decisions himself.

However, the Court of Appeal have taken a very narrow and restrictive approach to the case, particularly in the area of medical treatment. In *Re R. (A Minor) (Wardship: Medical Treatment)* (1992) the Court held that it had power under its parens patriae jurisdiction to override the decision of a competent child. It has used this power to set aside a child's refusal to treatment in *Re J. (A Minor) (Inherent Jurisdiction: Consent to Treatment)* (1992) (16 year old anorexic ordered to be fed) and in *Re E. (A Minor)* (1990) (ordering a blood transfusion despite 15 year old's religious objections).

These decisions have created considerable uncertainties. They dealt with a child's *refusal* to treatment: what would be the situation if the child *consented*, for example to an abortion, and the Court or the parents thought it in her best interests not to continue with the pregnancy? The uncertainties can only now be resolved by the House of Lords (or Parliament).

The Exercise of Parental Responsibility

By now, it will be appreciated that two or more persons may share parental responsibility. For example, parents married when the child was born share parental responsibility (see above). For example, a third party may obtain a court order one of the effects of which is to give him parental responsibility and, as this, save for an adoption order, does not terminate the parental responsibility of anyone who already has it (see above), shared parental responsibility will be created.

Section 2(7) provides that where parental responsibility is shared, each person having parental responsibility can act alone (subject to any enactment that provides for the consent of all on any specific issue).

Two general limitations to this freedom must be noted.

First, if there comes into existence an order under the CA (which determine the way in which some part of parental responsibility may be exercised), the persons having parental responsibility may not act in any way that is incompatible with it (s. 2(8)). For example, the court can grant a residence order under the CA, an order determining with whom the child is to live. If such an order is made, then a person with parental responsibility, who is not named in the order, can no longer exercise his parental responsibility by having the child live with him.

Secondly, despite section 2(7), it may be impossible in practice for one person with parental responsibility to exercise it without the co-operation of others with whom he shares it. For example, in practice, a married but separated father will find it impossible to exercise most aspects of his parental responsibility without the agreement of his wife, if the child lives with her. He will need the intervention of the court, thus bringing into play section 2(8).

CHILDREN OF THE FAMILY

By section 105, the term a child of the family, "in relation to the parties to a marriage, means:

(a) a child of both parties
(b) any other child, not being a child who is placed with the parties as foster parents . . . who has been treated by both of the parties as a child of their family."

This definition appears also in the M.C.A. and the D.P.M.C.A.

It will be seen that this is a relationship between a child and adults who are married to each other. The adults could be the child's natural parents but they need not be. One of the adults could be a parent and the other not: or both adults could have no blood tie with the child at all.

The relationship is of significance in that financial awards can be made in favour of such a child against the adults (Chapter 4). The relationship does not result in the adults having parental responsibility for the child; if the adults, or one of them, are the child's parents, they or he will have parental responsibility due to parenthood not as a result of the child being a child of the family. But the existence of this relationship does give adults who are not the child's parents some preferential treatment: they are entitled to apply for some of the CA orders (see Chapter 6).

Where it is necessary to prove that a child has been "treated as a child of the family," the issue is a question of fact to be viewed objectively. But there must be a family in existence before a child can be so treated:

A. v. *A.* (H.C. 1974)

Prior to the marriage, the wife falsely told the husband that the child she was carrying was his. They married but parted before the child's birth.

Held: the child was not a child of the family.

PRINCIPLES USED BY THE COURTS TO DETERMINE DISPUTES

The Non-Intervention Principle

Perhaps the most fundamental of all principles used by the courts to determine disputes is the principle that may result in a court not determining the dispute in any substantive way at all.

By section 1(5), the court is enjoined not to make an order under the CA unless it considers that doing so would be better for the child than making no order at all. (This principle does not therefore seem to apply to the decision as to whether to grant an adoption order or an order warding the child, neither of which are made under the C.A.)

This is a new principle, introduced to the statute book by the CA. Research had indicated that the grant of court orders relating to the upbringing of children sometimes exacerbated the child's position rather than bettered it. In the divorce and other matrimonial courts, there was an extremely prevalent practice of making orders relating to the upbringing of children, even when the parties were not contesting the issues. This is thought to be partly to blame for children frequently having lost contact with the parent with whom they did not live. Such a parent, faced with an order, sometimes "gave up" and failed even to exercise those parental rights left to him by the order. Further, the care of children was sometimes too precipitously transferred from their parents to local authorities by the courts.

While the possibility of granting orders relating to the upbringing of children recognises that court intervention will be necessary on occasion, the non-intervention principle places a statutory "brake" upon it.

The Paramountcy Principle

When determining any question relating to a child's upbringing or the administration of his property or income, the child's welfare is the court's paramount consideration (s. 1(1)).

Birmingham City Council v. H. (A minor)(No2) (1993)

The Local Authority had taken into care a child, aged 2, whose mother, aged 16, was also in care, and proposed to terminate contact, contrary to the wishes of the mother. The House of Lords held unanimously that the childs welfare was paramount and for the purpose of these proceedings the mother was to be treated as the parent, not as another child who was also subject to the welfare principle.

This principle is very similar to the principle that controlled such questions prior to the operative date of the CA: that the child's welfare should be the court's first and paramount consideration.

It will be noted that the word "first" is missing from the new formulation. In fact, it was the use of this word in earlier legislation that had caused difficulties. Here is Lord McDermott's attempt to define the meaning of "first and paramount" in *J*. v. *C*. (H.L. 1969).

> "The words must mean more than that the child's welfare is to be treated as the top item in a list of items relevant to the matter in question. I think that they connote a process whereby when all relevant facts, relationships, claims and wishes of the parents, risks, choices and other circumstances are taken into account and weighed, the course to be followed will be that which is most in the interests of the child's welfare as that term has now to be understood. That is the first consideration because it is of first importance and the paramount consideration because it rules on or determines the course to be followed."

With the advent of the CA, the difficulty of reconciling the word "first" with the word "paramount" disappears. Arguably, section 1(1), drawing on Lord McDermott's definition, means that the child's welfare is the determining or ruling factor, when dealing with questions relating to his upbringing or property.

Prior to the enactment of the CA, there were several types of proceedings the outcome of which affect the future of children, but which were held to be proceedings that did not relate to the "upbringing of children" and thus were not subject to the principle that their welfare was the court's first and paramount consideration. For example, the principle was not relevant in proceedings to obtain an order that a parent leave the home (see Chapter 5). It is suggested that the paramountcy principle is likely to be equally inapplicable in such proceedings in the future.

The Statutory List of Guidelines

While of immense importance, the principle contained in section 1(1) is very widely drawn. For more specific guidance, the courts must take into account the statutory list of guidelines contained in section 1(3), which, by and large, enacts in statutory form the principles developed previously by the courts in case law.

The list is as follows:

(a) the ascertainable wishes and feelings of the child (considered in the light of his age and understanding)—If at all, these used to be ascertained by a welfare officer, who had been ordered to prepare a report for the court

(b) his physical, emotional and educational needs—Courts have long been influenced by the idea that a child's development is assisted by maintaining a relationship with both parents, if possible. However, this has usually been achieved by the courts ordering that a child should live with one parent and have frequent and regular contact with the other. Only exceptionally, have courts ordered the child to live with one for part of the time and the other for the rest.

Also, generally, it has not been considered beneficial to grant an order the effect of which would have been to split siblings

(c) the likely effect on him of any change in his circumstances— Stability in the life of a child is considered beneficial. Thus, generally, a court has leant against an order the effect of which would have been to change well-established and beneficial arrangements, *e.g.* a change of home; a change of carer

> *Re H.* (*A Minor*) (*Custody: Interim Care and Control*) (C.A. 1991). A divorced mother had died and her daughter, aged eight, was with the maternal grandmother. The trial judge had ordered the child to be returned to the father but the Appeal Court held that she would stay with the grandmother for the time being until a full investigation be completed. It was important for her to be close to the mother's relatives in the early stages of bereavement. Approved in *Re W.* (*Residence Order*) (C.A. 1993)

(d) his age, sex, background and any characteristics of his which the court considers relevant—On the whole, courts have tended to consider that children need their mothers, young ones and girls in particular.

In *Re W.* (*A Minor*) (*Residence Order*) (C.A. 1992) the Court was prepared to say that there was a rebuttable presumption that a baby's best interest was to be with the mother. But in contrast, *Re S.* (*A Minor*) (*Custody*) (C.A.

1991) it was held that there was no presumption that one parent should be preferred to another

(e) any harm he has suffered or is at risk of suffering—Likely physical harm is obviously relevant but so is emotional harm. Thus, a parent's religious views or sexual preferences have been relevant if the court felt that they would damage the child

(f) how capable each of his parents, and any other person in relation to whom the court considers the question to be relevant, is of meeting his needs—This factor has been considered relevant in relation to any new partner of the parents or other persons who would take a large part in the upbringing of the child

(g) the range of powers available to the court under the CA in the proceedings in question.

These factors must be taken into account by all courts when considering an application for the grant, variation or discharge of a section 8 order (see Chapter 7) or an order under Part IV of the CA (see Chapter 8). Depending on the nature of the proceedings, some will be given more weight than others.

Delay

By section 1(2), the courts must take into account the principle that delay in resolving any dispute is likely to be prejudicial to a child.

CHILDREN'S RIGHTS

For centuries, children have been regarded as little better than the chattels of their parents. With a very few limitations, generally imposed by the criminal law, a child's welfare went unprotected: far less was he given the right to determine his own future, or even any say in the questions that concerned him. Today, the law no longer regards a child purely as a chattel; a number of legal developments have been responsible for this change, notably the juristic shift from parental rights to parental responsibility referred to above, the introduction of the paramountcy principle and the creation of local authority powers for the protection of children. However, the law still does not regard a child as an individual who has the same rights as an adult to determine his future.

Clearly, there are immense practical and legal problems in simply giving a child the right to determine issues that concern him. Perhaps the issue for the future is the balance to be struck between protection of a child's welfare on the one hand and a recognition of his rights on the other. As Lord Justice Butler Sloss said in the Report of the Inquiry into Child Abuse in Cleveland in 1987:

"There is a danger that in looking to the welfare of the children believed to be the victims of . . . abuse, the children themselves will be overlooked. The child is a person and not an object of concern."

Despite the heavy emphasis in the current law on the role that adults play in the lives of children, there have already been a number of moves to acknowledge that children have a role to play in their own lives.

The case of *Gillick* v. *West Norfolk Area Health Authority & Another* has already been referred to above. The Lords therein acknowledged that in some circumstances a child had the right to determine whether or not she should have contraceptive advice and treatment and in language that indicated that children possibly had other rights too.

However, the CA itself contains a number of provisions that acknowledge the role of children in their own lives. For example, a child's wishes and feelings are one of the factors listed in section 1(3): for example, a child may, with leave, apply for some CA orders in respect of himself: and, for example, a child may refuse to submit to a medical examination directed by the court, when granting an emergency protection order (see Chapter 8) (s. 44(7)).

---

7. RESOLUTION OF DISPUTES CONCERNING THE UPBRINGING OF CHILDREN BETWEEN PRIVATE INDIVIDUALS

Prior to the CA, the law was extremely complex. There was a wide variety of jurisdictions available, each relating to a specific situation, with its own procedures and types of orders. Further, the legal effect of the orders available was often unclear. The CA is designed to eradicate the complexity and uncertainty, yet still retain the flexibility, of the old law. In this chapter, reference to section numbers are to those in the CA, unless otherwise stated.

TYPES OF ORDERS

Save for adoption and an order warding a child, all orders that related to the upbringing of children have been swept away by the C.A. It is now no longer possible to obtain custody orders (sole, joint or split), care and control orders, access orders, custodianship orders or parental rights orders. A new guardianship scheme has been created by the CA, ss. 5 & 6: a new parental responsibility order for unmarried fathers has been created: most important, there are four new orders, created by the CA, s. 8 and referred to in that Act as "Section 8 orders." They are:

1. a residence order
2. a contact order
3. a prohibited steps order
4. a specific issues order.

The Residence Order

This is an order settling the arrangements to be made as to the person with whom the child is to live. It can be made in favour of anyone, save for a local authority. It can also be made in favour of more than one person, and if it is and those persons do not live together, then the order may specify the periods of time the child is to spend with each of the persons named in the order.

It will frequently be the case that a residence order is granted to a person who already has parental responsibility for the child, *e.g.* a married parent. If this is *not* the case, the legal effect of the residence order is to give the person named in the order the parental responsibility for the child, save that such a person cannot consent to adoption or an order freeing for adoption or appoint a guardian (s. 12). Such parental responsibility lasts as long as the residence order remains in force.

Obtaining a residence order is one way therefore for non parents to obtain the parental responsibility (or at least the large part of it), for a child. If this happens however, remember that this does not destroy the parental responsibility that other persons—*e.g.* the parents—already have (s. 2(6)): it means simply that they cannot act in any way that is incompatible with the residence order (s. 2(8)).

The Contact Order

This is an order requiring the person with whom the child lives to allow the child to visit or stay, or otherwise have contact, with the person(s) named in the order. Again, it can be made in favour of anyone, save for a local authority. The term "or otherwise have contact with" is capable of wide interpretation and could include for example writing to or receiving letters from, or making or receiving telephone calls to or from, the named person.

The Prohibited Steps Order

This is an order directing a person named in the order not to take a specified step in relation to the child without the consent of the court. It can be made against anyone.

The "specified step" must be one which could be taken by a parent in meeting his parental responsibility. Thus, for example, any person could be directed not to make arrangements for, or consent to, an operation on the child, such steps being examples of those that could be taken by a parent in meeting his parental responsibility. But the courts could not, for example, use this order against a newspaper to prevent the publication of material relating to a child, such a step probably not being one that could be taken by a parent in the exercise of his parental responsibility.

The Specific Issues Order

This is an order that determines a specific question in connection with any aspect of parental responsibility, for example which school the child should attend, which religion he should be brought up in.

Neither the prohibited steps order nor the specific issues order can be made with a view to achieving a result which could be achieved by the making of a residence or contact order (s. 9(5)). If this provision were not on the statute book, a person could feasibly avoid the legal effect of the residence or contact order by seeking a specific issue or prohibited steps order to cover the same situation.

All section 8 orders can be made subject to directions as to their implementation and conditions that must be complied with (s. 11(7)). For example, it would be possible to grant a person a residence order subject to the condition that he lived in a named town; or subject to a condition that he provide regular reports on the progress of the child at school to some other person. For example, the contact order could include precise directions as to the place, manner and time of the visits.

None of these orders can be made once the child has reached his 16th birthday or extend beyond that date, unless there are exceptional circumstances (s. 9(6)&(7)). In any event, all of these orders cease automatically when the child reaches 18 (s. 91(11)).

TYPES OF PROCEEDINGS

Disputes concerning the upbringing of children can arise in many ways. The adults in dispute could be in dispute solely over the upbringing of the child: or they may also be in dispute about other matters (*e.g.* divorce) that can be conveniently linked with the dispute over the child. Under the old law, it was possible to deal with the issue relating to the child as a separate issue, under the Guardianship of Minors Act 1971. But it was also possible to obtain orders relating to children under other jurisdictions, thereby linking the issue relating to the child with other issues. Unfortunately, while this created flexibility, it also created an extremely complex situation. Each jurisdiction had its own different rules, conditions and powers.

The complexity is greatly eradicated by the C A. This Act sweeps away virtually all the mass of diverse statutory provisions relating to the upbringing of children. Now, the only way for private individuals to take the initiative to resolve a dispute concerning the upbringing of a child is for one of them to issue proceedings under the C.A. The only exceptions relate to wardship and adoption orders.

Under the CA, it is possible to apply for an order appointing a guardian of the child (s. 5), such an order giving parental responsibility. It is also possible for an unmarried father to apply for an order giving him parental responsibility (s. 4—see Chapter 6). However, the main type of application possible is for a section 8 order.

An application for a section 8 order can be made in one of two ways:

1. as a free standing application (s. 10(2))
2. as part of "family proceedings" (s. 10(1)).

"Family proceedings" are defined in section 8. The list includes jurisdictions which used to have their own powers to grant orders relating to the upbringing of children, *e.g.* the M.C.A., and the D.P.M.C.A. It also includes other jurisdictions, *e.g.* the D.V.A. and the M.H.A. Further, it includes applications under Part 1 of the CA itself. For example, if an unmarried father applies for an order giving him parental responsibility under section 4, section 8 orders can be sought within the section 4 proceedings.

This dual approach retains (and extends) the flexibility of the old law. The issue relating to the child can be dealt with on its own, if this is the only issue in dispute. Or it can be dealt with together with other issues, if that is what is needed. The difference is that the jurisdiction and powers of the court are the same, no matter whether the application is made under section 10(1) or (2) and, if within family proceedings under section 10(1), no matter which type.

It should also be noted that once family proceedings are issued, the court can make a section 8 order of its own motion (s. 10(1)).

CATEGORIES OF APPLICANTS

Usually, it is the parents of a child who are in dispute about his upbringing. However, this is not always necessarily so; a person who has no relationship whatsoever with the child may still have a genuine interest in his welfare and require an order relating to his upbringing.

There were jurisdictions under which persons who were not the parents of the child were entitled to apply for orders relating to the child's upbringing. However, there were elements of control too: each jurisdiction had its own qualifying conditions and, if a person could not satisfy any of these, then his only recourse was the wardship jurisdiction, which did, and still does, permit any person to ward a child (see Chapter 8).

The CA recognises the need for persons other than parents of a child to be able to obtain orders relating to his upbringing. It would have been possible to provide that any one was entitled to apply for a section 8 order. However, this freedom was not

considered appropriate and the CA lays down categories of applicant in section 10.

1. Those entitled to apply for any section 8 order:
   - (i) a parent or guardian of the child (it need not be a parent with parental responsibility)
   - (ii) a person who has been granted a residence order.
2. Those entitled to apply for a residence or contact order:
   - (i) a spouse or ex-spouse in relation to whom the child is a child of the family (see Chapter 6)
   - (ii) a person with whom the child has lived for at least three years. Section 10(10) provides that this need not be continuous, so long as the period does not commence more than five years, nor end more than three months before, the making of the application.
   - (iii) a person who has the consent of
     - (a) the person in whose favour there is a residence order, if one has been granted
     - (b) the local authority, if the child is in care
     - (c) in any other case, every person with parental responsibility.
3. Any other person who has leave of the court to make the application.

The matters which a court must take into account on an application for leave are designed to prevent frivolous and/or harmful
applications for section 8 orders being made. They include the
nature of the applicant's connection with the child (s. 10(9)) but
as it is not "a question with respect to the upbringing of the
child", his or her welfare is not a paramount consideration. An
unusual example is:

Re A. and others (Minors) (Residence orders: Leave to Apply) (C.A. 1992)

Six disturbed children (aged 9–14) had been taken into care and placed
with an experienced but strong-minded foster mother. The arrangement
worked for two years, then the two elder children ran away. The other
four were taken for assessment, then placed with another foster family.
The first foster mother applied for leave to apply for residence orders.
The Court of Appeal refused. The court could assume that the Local
Authority were safeguarding the children's welfare; they and the natural
mother opposed the application, the children did not want to go back,
and no point would be served in a lengthy and bitter court battle.

THE RELATIONSHIP BETWEEN THE PRIVATE AND THE PUBLIC LAW

In Chapter 8, there is discussed the topic of protection of a child by local authority intervention in his life. This topic can no longer be studied as if it were a completely separate topic from the law discussed in this chapter: the two interweave.

As seen above, two of the section 8 orders, the specific issue order and the prohibited steps order can be granted in favour of a local authority.

Further, as will be seen in Chapter 8, a local authority can apply for care or supervision orders, under Part IV of the C A. Such an application is included in the definition of "family proceedings." Thus, if such an application is initiated, an application for a section 8 order can be made, or the court can make a section 8 order of its own motion, within it.

The circle does not end here however: as will be seen, applications for care and supervision orders can be made within family proceedings. Thus, a private individual who has instituted some form of family proceedings in which a question relating to a child arises, may find a local authority applying within them for care or supervision.

This interweaving is an attempt to ensure that the courts have the powers to resolve an issue relating to a child in the most appropriate way, without being limited by the identity of the applicant or the nature of the order sought.

Nottinghamshire County Council v. *P.* (1993)

> The Local Authority were criticised by the Court of Appeal for seeking section 8 orders in an alleged sexual abuse case: care or supervision orders would have provided the appropriate remedy.

FACTORS TAKEN INTO ACCOUNT WHEN DETERMINING DISPUTES

These have already been discussed in Chapter 6.

8. PROTECTION OF CHILDREN—LOCAL AUTHORITY INTERVENTION AND WARDSHIP

Occasionally, the state is forced to intervene between a child and its carers, either to remove the child completely from the home or to provide some form of intermediate protection. Usually the protection is achieved by means of local authority intervention in the life of the child, but protection can also be given by making a child a ward of court. References in this chapter to section numbers are to those in the CA, unless otherwise stated.

TYPES OF ORDERS

Prior to the enactment of the CA, there were many different types of orders available to a local authority to enable it to offer protection to a child. A local authority could also pass a resolution assuming the parental rights relating to a child. Further, prior to the CA, there was great uncertainty concerning the legal effect of the orders and resolution and the powers thereby given to a local authority.

The CA attempts to eradicate the uncertainty of the old law. In addition, it sweeps away all of the orders that gave a local authority powers over children and replaces them with a new scheme to be found only in the Act. It must be said that the range of orders available to a local authority is still wide. This does, however, offer a very flexible response to a child in need of protection. It should also be noted that a local authority can no longer pass a parental rights resolution relating to a child: no child may now be taken into care without a court order.

The orders that are now available are as follows:

1. the care order (s. 31)
2. the supervision order (s. 31)
3. the education supervision order (s. 36)
4. the emergency protection order (s. 44)
5. the child assessment order (s. 43).

The Care Order

This is an order that commits a child into the care of a local authority. It cannot be made in favour of anyone else.

The practical effect of a care order is that the child goes to live in a local authority community home or with local authority foster parents.

The legal effect of a care order is that the local authority obtains parental responsibility for the child so long as the care order is in force (s. 33(3)). It cannot, however, cause the child to be brought up in any religious persuasion other than that in which he would have been brought up if the order had not been made. Nor can it consent to an order for adoption or freeing for adoption or appoint a guardian (s. 33(6)).

A care order automatically brings to an end any residence order that is in existence, and with it any parental responsibility that it gave (s. 91(2)). But if a parent (natural or adoptive), or guardian, has parental responsibility at the time that a care order comes into force, this continues (s. 2(6)). However, such a person is not entitled to exercise it in any way incompatible with the care order (s. 2(8)) and, further, the local authority may determine the extent to which such a person may exercise his parental responsibility.

A care order cannot be made in respect of a child who has reached the age of 17 (16, if the child is married). It lasts until the child is 18, unless it is discharged earlier.

The Supervision Order

This is an order placing a child under the supervision of a local authority or probation officer. The supervision order does not give the supervising authority the parental responsibility for the child and the child cannot be removed from his home. The supervising authority merely has the duty to "advise, assist and befriend" the child, which it will do in any way it considers appropriate, *e.g.* by visiting the child regularly. A supervision order can have conditions attached to it, *e.g.* directing the participation of the child in specified activities.

Clearly, the supervision order is an intermediate means of protection for a child. However, if the supervising authority considers that the order is not being fully complied with, it must consider applying for its variation or discharge and, if the latter, may also consider applying for a care order.

A supervision order cannot be made in respect of a child who has reached the age of 17 (16, if the child is married). Generally, a supervision order lasts for one year. It can be extended for up to a further two years. In any event, it cannot extend beyond the child's 18th birthday.

The Education Supervision Order

This is an order placing a child under the supervision of a local education authority. Like the supervision order, it does not give the authority parental responsibility for the child.

The Emergency Protection Order

Proceedings for the orders previously referred to will usually take some time to conclude. Some children require protection more quickly and the emergency protection order is designed to fulfil this need.

It is an order that authorises a local authority (or the N.S.P.C.C.) to remove a child from his home and gives it parental responsibility. Regulations provide that an application for an emergency protection order can be made "ex parte"; that is, without the necessity to inform the child's parents or any other person that the application is about to be made. Thus, it will be possible to obtain the order very swiftly indeed and after the court has heard only the local authority's side of the case.

This order is obviously a very drastic remedy. To counter balance this, the order lasts for a very limited period, eight days, and can only be extended once by a further period not exceeding seven days. Further, after 72 hours, an application for its discharge can be made (s. 45(1)(5)(6) & (9)). In addition, it is specifically provided that the local authority shall only take such action in meeting its parental responsibility as is reasonably required to safeguard or promote the welfare of the child (s. 44(5)).

The Child Assessment Order

The orders that are referred to above in effect replace orders that were available under previous legislation, albeit in an improved fashion. The child assessment order is a new concept.

Sometimes, a local authority fears that a child may be at immediate risk, yet, because it cannot gain access to the child, has no real evidence of the fact or extent of the risk. In the past, it has had two alternatives: either to apply for a place of safety order (the old rough equivalent of the emergency protection order) and immediately remove the child from its home, or to do nothing.

This led to place of safety orders being granted on flimsy evidence, and children being removed from their homes in situations where it was later discovered they need not have been, or alternatively, children suffering harm. The child assessment order is designed to provide a solution to this dilemma.

The child assessment order has effect for no more than seven days (s. 43(5)) and authorises either a local authority or the N.S.P.C.C. to carry out an assessment on the child (s. 43(7)). Any person who is in a position to produce the child for assessment must do so (s. 43(6)). To give added strength to the order, it is provided that a child assessment order may permit the removal of the child from his home (s. 43(9)). The child assessment order does not give the local authority or the N.S.P.C.C. parental responsibility for the child.

The intention behind the order is to enable the local authority to assess the child, so that it can better make its decision as to whether to apply for one of the more drastic orders, yet, at the same time, cause the minimum harm to the child.

TYPES OF PROCEEDINGS

Prior to the enactment of the CA, it was possible to make orders giving a local authority the right to intervene in a child's life under a number of different jurisdictions, some of which were at least in part overlapping, but which had their own criteria to be fulfilled. This complexity has been addressed by the C A. Subject to a very limited use of the wardship jurisdiction (see below), the CA is now the only jurisdiction under which a local authority may intervene in the life of a child.

However, a certain amount of flexibility is retained, by sometimes permitting the use of the same device as has been discussed in Chapter 7. By section 31(4), an application for a care order or a supervision order can be made on its own or within family proceedings, as defined by section 8(3) (see Chapter 7). However, applications for education supervision orders, emergency protection orders and child assessment orders may only be made as free standing applications and not within family proceedings.

CATEGORIES OF APPLICANT

The wide scope that prevails within the sphere of resolution of private disputes was not thought appropriate for this area and the categories of persons who are entitled to apply for the above orders for the protection of children are extremely limited.

Care orders, supervision orders and child assessment orders— only a local authority or the N.S.P.C.C. may apply.

Education supervision orders—only a local education authority may apply.

Emergency protection orders—any person may apply. (The emergency nature and limited life of this order should be remembered. In practice, it will most often be sought by a local authority.)

Further it has been considered correct not to re-enact the court's previous powers to make orders for the protection of children of its own motion. Thus, even if a court dealing with family proceedings (*e.g.* divorce) feels that, *e.g.* a care order should be made in respect of a child, it cannot make such an order unless the local authority applies for one within those proceedings.

In place of the previous powers to make orders of its own motion, the court now has more intermediate powers under section 37. Where a court is dealing with family proceedings in which a question relating to the welfare of a child arises, it may direct a local authority to investigate the child's circumstances, if it appears that a care or supervision order may be appropriate. Once so directed, a local authority has the duty to carry out an investigation, and to consider, *inter alia*, whether it should apply for a care or supervision order. If it decides not to, a local authority must report this to the court. However, there is nothing the court can do to reverse the local authority decision.

THE RELATIONSHIP BETWEEN THE PUBLIC AND PRIVATE LAW

As has been stated earlier, care and supervision orders can be sought by a local authority and granted, within proceedings initially instituted by a private individual to resolve a dispute between himself and another private individual, so long as such proceedings fall within the definition of family proceedings.

Further, what by now may have been forgotten, is that a local authority may, with leave, apply for and be granted a specific issue order or a prohibited steps order, either as a free standing application or within family proceedings (see Chapter 7).

Finally, applications for care orders, supervision orders and education supervision orders are themselves "family proceedings" (s. 8(4)). Thus, whenever such an application is made, the applicant (the local authority, N.S.P.C.C. or education local authority) must face the fact that the court has the power to grant a specific issue order or prohibited steps order instead of the order sought, or indeed, a section 8 order to a private individual.

GROUNDS

Care and Supervision Orders (s. 31(2))

The court has to be satisfied

   (a) that the child is suffering or likely to suffer significant harm and
   (b) that the harm or likelihood of harm is attributable to
      (i) the care given to the child, or likely to be given to him if the order were not made, not being what it would be reasonable to expect a parent to give to him or
     (ii) the child's being beyond parental control.

"Harm" is defined in section 31(9) as "ill treatment, or the impairment of health or development" and those terms are defined in the same subsection. In short, it is not only the child's physical well being that is protected. It is further provided that, where the harm alleged is "impairment of health or development," whether or not it is significant shall be decided by using the standard of the health or development to be reasonably expected of a similar child (s. 31(10)).

Proof of the ground in section 31(2) only entitles a court to grant a care or supervision order. The court does not have to: indeed before it does, there are other matters that it must take into account, that may lead it to refuse a care or supervision order. As a result, the grounds specified in section 31(2) are popularly known as the "threshold grounds."

The whole of section 1 applies to care and supervision proceedings. This is discussed in Chapter 6 under the heading "Principles to be applied by the courts when determining disputes."

Education Supervision Orders (s. 36(3) & (4))

The court has to be satisfied that the child is of compulsory school age and is not being properly educated: *i.e.* receiving efficient full-time education, suitable to his age, ability, aptitude and any special education needs he may have.

Again, proof of this ground can be looked upon as having reached a threshold only. Applications for education supervision orders are subject to the whole of section 1.

Emergency Protection Orders (s. 44(1))

Three situations are catered for under the CA: applications made by a local authority or the N.S.P.C.C., where either of them is already making enquiries into a child's welfare, and any other application. To summarise:

(a) a local authority, already making enquiries, must show merely that the enquiries are being frustrated and that access to the child is required as a matter of urgency

(b) the N.S.P.C.C., already making enquiries, must show the matters mentioned in (a), plus that it has reasonable cause to suspect that the child is suffering, or likely to suffer, significant harm

(c) any other applicant must show that there is reasonable cause to believe that the child is likely to suffer significant harm if he is not removed to other accommodation.

Again, proof of the ground can be looked upon as having reached a threshold only. Applications for emergency protection orders are subject to the provisions of section 1, *save for section 1(3)*, the statutory list of guidelines. It will be remembered that these orders are for the emergency protection of children: it was not thought appropriate to insist that the courts should take note of these matters on what were likely to be speedy applications.

Child Assessment Orders (s. 43(1))

To summarise, the court has to be satisfied that:

(a) the applicant has reasonable cause to suspect that the child is suffering or likely to suffer significant harm

(b) this can only be determined by an assessment of the child's health or development and

(c) it is not likely that an assessment will be made without an order.

Again, proof of the ground can be regarded as having reached a threshold only. Applications for child assessment orders are subject to the provisions of section 1, *save for section 1(3)*. Such applications are, again, emergency applications.

PARENTAL CONTACT

One of the severest criticisms of the law prior to the CA was that it gave a local authority an almost completely free hand in determining the extent to which a child in care could have contact with his parents. This has been remedied.

By section 34, a local authority is placed under a duty to allow reasonable contact between a child in care and, *inter alia*, his parents. If there is a dispute as to what is reasonable, then the court can make such order for contact as it considers appropriate. In limited circumstances, a local authority can refuse to permit contact, for up to seven days.

By section 43, if a child is to be kept away from his home during the currency of a child assessment order, the order must contain directions for such contact between the child and other persons as the court thinks fit.

By section 44, an applicant who is granted an emergency protection order is placed under a duty to allow reasonable contact between the child, and *inter alia*, his parents.

WARDSHIP

Wardship is the means by which the family court fulfils its *parens patriae* jurisdiction, that is, the protection of children.

When a child becomes a ward of court, the Court controls its upbringing by a series of directions and orders of the widest variety so long as the wardship lasts. Wardship not only deals with the issues of where and with whom a child shall live, but also with important other issues, for example, consenting to an operation to remove a potentially fatal intestinal blockage (*Re B*. (C.A. 1981)): to perform an abortion (*Re P*. (H.C. 1986)): to decide whether to prolong a dying baby's life or to ease his suffering (*Re C*. (C.A. 1989)).

The flexibility of wardship also appealed Local Authorities who often chose this jurisdiction in preference to care proceedings. The result was a dramatic increase in the number of cases during the two decades preceding the C A.

However, by section 100 of the CA, no local authority may apply to make a child a ward of court unless it has leave of the Court to do so. The grounds for leave are so limited that it seems wardship will be used in only the most exceptional circumstances. Indeed, recent cases seem to point to the success of the multiplicity of orders available under the CA, for example, *Re H.G.* (*Specific Issue: Sterilisation*) (1993) and *Re R.* (*A Minor*) (*Blood Transfusion*) (1993). In the area of private law, the reduction in Legal Aid limits is likely to affect the number of applications, particularly as section 8 orders are available in the lower courts. Nonetheless, the immediacy of wardship and its ability to deal with unusual, if not unique, situations, means that wardship still has a role to play in child law.

X County Council v. *A.* (1985)

A notorious murderer, on release from prison, had changed her name and gone to live in a different part of the country. She had her child warded so that the Court could order the News of the World not to publish any material which would identify either mother or child.

Devon County Council v. *S. (Wardship)* (1993)

S. had three young children. She was regularly visited by X. who had convictions for sexual offences. The local authority applied for wardship to protect the children. The trial judge refused, relying on section 10 but leave was granted by the Court of Appeal to enable contact between X. and the children to be prevented, something which care or supervision orders could not achieve.

9. QUESTIONS

1. Compare and contrast the powers of the magistrates' court to deal with domestic violence under the D.P.M.C.A. 1978 with the powers of the county court under the D.V.A. 1976.

What proposals for reform does the Law Commission suggest in its working paper No. 113?

2. Harry (H.) and Wilma (W.) married seven years ago. They have no children. Within a year of the marriage, W. began to show signs of a severe personality disorder and mental illness. As a result, W. became averse to life with H. She went out frequently without him, sometimes staying away overnight, associated with numerous other men, occasionally had sexual intercourse with them, and boasted of it afterwards to H. When he remonstrated with her, she became abusive. When at home, W. spent much of her time locked in the spare bedroom and often failed to do any housework or cooking. Eventually she began to go out less and less and her lack of interest in H. became a lack of interest in herself.

Two years ago, W. was admitted to a mental hospital. During the first six months, H. was keen to keep the marriage alive, visited her regularly and W. came home for a week at a time on six occasions. However, W.'s illness became worse and the parties have not seen each other since then. H. wants a divorce and W., when she will speak at all, says she wants one too. W.'s doctors think that this may aid her recovery.

Can H. petition for divorce?

3. Mike (M.), a builder and Winnie (W.), a teacher, have never married. When they met, four years ago, M. had found a house which required renovation but was unable to raise enough money to buy it. W. gave him £5,000 to make up the deposit and M. signed a document in which he agreed to repay the money within five years. The house was purchased in M.'s name alone.

Soon afterwards, the parties decided to set up home with each other. They talked about their future and agreed that the property should be a "joint effort." W. helped considerably with the renovation by labouring at the property. She used her salary to buy food and clothing, to pay for the parties' holidays and to buy furniture and fitting for the property. Occasionally, she paid some of the mortgage instalments. M. used the income he saved to renovate the property to a higher standard and, once the renovation was complete, to take up power boat racing.

Two years ago, W. gave birth to their child and stopped work. The relationship deteriorated and M. left W. a week ago. She has now received a letter from M., enclosing a cheque for £5,000, in "repayment of the loan" and asking her to leave his house.

Does W. have an interest in the house and, if so, what is its extent?

4. C., a girl aged 14, has been raped and is now 10 weeks pregnant. She is naturally suffering from severe shock and will not talk about her situation with anyone, save to say that she wants an abortion. Since the divorce of her parents, C. has lived with her mother, Mrs. X., but sees her father, Mr. X., regularly. On the divorce, a residence order was made in favour of Mrs. X. Mrs. X. has deep rooted objections to abortion: Mr. X. does not.

Is it necessary to obtain Mrs. X.'s consent to an abortion on C.?

5. Wilma (W.) met Harry (H.) five years ago, and shortly afterwards she moved from her home town 200 miles away, to go and live with him. She took with her Daphne, her two year old daughter by a previous relationship. The parties have a three year old son, Samuel. W. does not work. H. is a prosperous business man. Both the legal and beneficial interests in their home belong to H.

What rights of occupation in it does W. have, or may she obtain, on the breakdown of her relationship with H.:

   (a) if she is married to H.?
   (b) if she is not?

6. Chris and Gaby were married in 1990. After several miscarriages, Gaby was told she could not carry a child full term. Chris and Gaby then entered into an agreement with Gaby's married sister, Kathy, that Kathy would bear a child for £10,000 expenses. An egg from Gaby was fertilised by Chris, the resulting embryo was then implanted and carried full term by Kathy. Immediately after the birth of the child, Kathy took him to Chris and Gaby. A year later, Chris and Gaby were divorced on the grounds of her adultery with Danny. The baby still lives with Gaby. Danny has applied for a residence order. Kathy and her husband, and Chris, all want the child to live with them.

Advise the parties.

7. Harry (H.), aged 63, has been married to Wilma (W.), aged 45, for 25 years. Last week he left her and went to live with a

lady with whom he has been having an affair for some three years. H. has no complaints to make against W. but he says the marriage is over and he wants a divorce as soon as possible. W. does not want a divorce. Her religious beliefs are against divorce and, further, she says that she would suffer financially, as she would lose the chance to benefit from H.'s occupational pension schemes, as his widow, should he die first.

(a) **Advise H.**
(b) **Would your advice be different if the proposals of the Law Commission, contained in its Report on the Ground for Divorce, No. 192, were now law?**

8. "The local authorities' social workers . . . are in an invidious position: great responsibilities (towards children) . . . but, as some would say, inadequate legal powers to discharge those responsibilities. And so it has become . . . quite frequent for local authorities nowadays to resort to the ward of court procedure to help them over their difficulties." Ormrod L.J. in *Re C.B.* (C.A. 1981).

To what extent is this an accurate statement of the law and local authority practice today?

9. "Although it is designed to benefit children, in both origin and intention, it was framed primarily to reduce expenditure". (Lord McGregor in the Report Stage of the Child Support Bill.)

Comment on this statement now that the C.S.A. has been fully implemented.

---

10. SUMMARY SUGGESTED ANSWERS

1. *Types of orders—*
—Describe the orders available in M.C. and C.C.
—Compare non-molestation injunction with the family protection order, with particular reference to definition of molestation in *Horner* v. *Horner*

—Compare exclusion from home in M.C. with ouster from home, part or area in C.C.

Identity of applicant and respondent—
—Both can entertain applications from spouses against spouses
—Refer to C.C. power to entertain application from "a man or woman who are living with each other in the same household as husband and wife" against other partner and compare with inability of M.C. to entertain such applications.

Factors considered by court in exercising jurisdiction—
—Describe factors in the D.P.M.C.A., s. 16(2) & (3). Describe factors in the M.H.A., s. 1(3), relevant to D.V.A. due to *Richards*
—Compare the need, generally, to establish violence or threat of it in the M.C. with its lack of predominance in the C.C.
—Once conditions in section 16(2) or (3) are fulfilled, is M.C. then bound by *Richards*?

Power of arrest—
—Describe the orders to which it can be attached in M.C. and C.C.
—Compare their different wordings
—Describe the conditions that must be fulfilled before it can be attached
—Compare their different wordings, physical injury as opposed to A.B.H., with particular reference to *Kendrick*.

Other differences:
E.g. persons protected by orders: powers in urgent cases.

Law Commission working paper No. 113: two possible models for reform of whole area of domestic violence:

1. replacing the present schemes with one new structure, in which individual courts may have different powers
2. leaving the present structure in place, but eradicating gaps, deficiencies and inconsistencies.

In either scheme, it will be necessary to address the issue of the extent of the powers to be given to the M.C. Many of the present limitations discussed above are deliberate, given the unqualified bench and summary procedure of the court: *e.g.* no power to grant orders to unmarried partners; no power to grant non-molestation orders; no power to grant exclusion from an area around the home.

However, some differences seem to have no political basis and could be eradicated: *e.g.* the M.C.'s lack of power to attach a power of arrest directly to an exclusion order; the M.C.'s power to attach a power of arrest only on proof of physical injury as opposed to A.B.H.; the case law criteria applicable in the C.C. for urgent cases as compared with that specified in section 16(8); whether section 1(3) of the M.H.A. applies to the M.C.

2. H. must establish that marriage has irretrievably broken down (M.C.A., s. 1(1)) by proving one of the five facts (M.C.A., s. 1(2)).

M.C.A., section 1(2)(d)

Have the parties "lived apart?" One of the parties must have had the required mental attitude, *i.e.* that the marriage was at an end (*Santos*). What is the effect of H.'s feelings when W. first hospitalised?

Has the separation been continuous and for two years? Continuity is not broken by period(s) of cohabitation of less than six months but such period(s) cannot be included in the calculation of the two year period (M.C.A., s. 2). What is the effect of W.'s home visits?

Has W. the mental capacity to give consent? W. must be capable of knowing that she is consenting to divorce and understanding the consequences (*Mason*).

M.C.A., section 1(2)(a)

Has W. committed adultery? Intercourse must have been willing. This assumes W. had the mental capacity to form the intent to commit adultery.

What is the effect of the parties having lived together after H. discovered W.'s adultery? Periods of cohabitation of more than six months will destroy H.'s right to rely on an incident of adultery. Periods of less than six months are ignored when assessing intolerability (M.C.A., s. 2). When did W. last commit adultery? Could the early part of W.'s hospitalisation count as "living together?" What is "living together?"

Does the adultery have to be the cause of the intolerability? Cleary.

M.C.A., section 1(2)(b)

What is behaviour? Livingstone-Stallard.

What behaviour can be alleged? Positive behaviour (W.'s abuse and associations short of adultery) and negative behaviour (W.'s failure to do housework and associate with H.) are both relevant (*Thurlow*). A "state of affairs" does not amount to behaviour (*Katz*). Can H. rely on W.'s hospitalisation?

Is W.'s mental illness relevant? W.'s lack of intention or capacity to form intent does not prevent her actions from constituting behaviour. The fact that W. is ill is relevant in assessing whether it is reasonable to expect H. to live with her.

3. *Establishing a trust*—W. must show either that parties expressly agreed that they were both beneficially entitled or that an inference that they both intended this can be drawn from their conduct. Further, in either case, W. must show that she acted to her detriment in reliance upon the agreement or common intent (*Lloyd's Bank PLC* v. *Rosset*).

Was there an express agreement? All depends upon the interpretation of the parties agreement that property was to be a "joint effort."

If so, has W. acted to her detriment? W. need not have made direct contributions to the purchase price of the property (*Lloyd's Bank PLC* v. *Rosset*). Indirect financial contributions that are "referable to the purchase of the property" or conduct that is "more than an ordinary wife would do" can be taken into account (*Grant* v. *Edwards: Eves*). Can W.'s payments for food, clothing, holidays and furniture be argued to be referable to the purchase of the property, in that not having to make such payments, M. was enabled to improve the property to a higher standard? Quare effect of those that enabled M. to take up power boat racing. W.'s extensive labouring at property may be taken to be more than an ordinary wife would do.

If not, was there a "common intent?" This can be inferred from direct
contributions to the purchase price, but possibly, from no other
conduct (*Lloyd's Bank PLC* v. *Rosset*). Arguably, W.'s initial contribution was a loan and thus irrelevant. Are her later occasional
payments of the mortgage enough? Must such contributions be
"substantial" (see, *e.g. Gissing*).

Quantification of shares—Again, W. must show an express agreement
or a common intent as to the size of her interest. It is possible
for the parties to have agreed or commonly intended an interest
that was to be quantified at a later date (*Stokes* v. *Anderson*).

If no agreement, what conduct suffices? See generally, *B.* v. *B.* Further,
the loan is relevant on this issue (*Risch* v. *McFee*).

4. *Does C. have the capacity to consent to the abortion herself?* F.L.R.A.
1969, s. 8 inapplicable, as C. is not 16 or over.
   A child under 16 has capacity to consent to medical treatment
in some circumstances (*Gillick*). Is C. "capable of understanding
what is proposed" and is the operation "what is best for her
welfare?" (Lord Fraser of Tullybelton). Is C. "of sufficient understanding and intelligence to enable her to fully understand what
is proposed?" (Lord Scarman). Does "the nature of the operation"
and C.'s "age and understanding" make C.'s consent effective?
(Lord Templeman). Note also the Court of Appeal's recent
criticism.
   How far, if at all, have these principles been affected by the
enactment of the CA?

Is Mr. X.'s consent sufficient? C. is a child born to married parents.
Her parents have joint parental responsibility (CA, s. 2(1)). Both
are entitled to act alone in meeting that P.R. (s. 2(7)), but neither
is entitled to act in any way incompatible with any order granted
under the CA (s. 2(8)). Mrs. X. has a residence order in her
favour, granted under the CA, s. 8, but this merely "settles the
arrangements as to the person with whom the child is to live."
At law therefore, Mr. X.'s consent to the operation is all that is
needed.
   However, C. lives with her mother and it may in practice be
impossible for Mr. X. to arrange for C. to have the operation.
   Mr. X. should seek a specific issue order under the CA, s. 8,
seeking the court's direction that C. should have an abortion. As
a parent, Mr. X., is entitled to apply for any section 8 order (s.

9(4)) and can do so within "family proceedings", *e.g.* the divorce proceedings, or by way of a free standing application (s. 10(1) & (2)).

If such an order is granted, Mrs. X. must not act in anyway incompatible with it (s. 2(8)).

5(a). *Rights under the M.H.A.* A non-owning spouse (W.) has statutory rights of occupation in the home when it belongs to the other (H.). Such rights last until the termination of the marriage, *e.g.* by divorce. Such rights are a charge on the property and will bind a purchaser if registered.

Rights under the M.C.A. On divorce, the court has the power, *inter alia*, to order one spouse to transfer property to the other or to settle property for the benefit of the other (s. 24).

The court could order H. to transfer the home outright to W., giving her exclusive rights of occupation. Alternatively, it could order a settlement that gave rights of occupation. Typical are a *Mesher order*—where W. gains exclusive occupation until the youngest child of the family reaches a stated age (only relevant where there are children)—and a *Martin order*—where W. gains exclusive occupation until her death or remarriage.

On application for a property adjustment order, the court must give first consideration to the welfare of Daphne and Samuel, the minor children of the family (s. 25). It must also take into account factors listed in s. 25(2). Here most relevant are:

  (i) W.'s lack of resources, both income and capital
  (ii) W.'s lack of earning capacity, having two young children
 (iii) H. is a prosperous business man
 (iv) W. has to house herself and two young children.

5(b). The M.H.A. and the M.C.A. do not apply.

Can W. prove H. granted her an irrevocable licence to occupy his premises? Did she give consideration? Is there evidence of an express agreement to this effect or can the terms of such a licence, particularly the duration, be inferred from the conduct of the parties (as in *Tanner*)? W.'s having given up her home to move to live with H. may well be relevant.

Rights under the D.V.A. If H. and W. are "living with each other in the same household as husband and wife" the court has the power to oust H. from the home.

In effect, such an order would give W. exclusive occupation but the D.V.A. is not designed to award or confirm *rights* of occupation; it provides short term protection, usually, but not exclusively, from violence. Such an order normally lasts only three months.

6. A complex question on parental responsibility (PR) and H.F.E.A. which needs a logical and sequential approach.

—Section 30 of the H.F.E.A. gives the Court power to order that the child is to be treated as a child of the married couple where a surrogate has entered into just such an arrangement. Must satisfy conditions:
—Couple must be married and over 18.
—Agreement made within six months of birth.
—Child must live with married couple.
—Carrying mother must consent.
—No money or benefit changed hands other than reasonable expenses.

If the above are satisfied, C.&G. become parents for the purposes of CA. Query if £10,000 is reasonable. If not, K. remains parent with PR.

If C.&G. acquire PR it is never lost despite divorce.

Section 8 orders can give PR to others, including D. if he obtains a residence order. But he must satisfy conditions, *e.g.* as a step-parent.
If section 30 of the H.F.E.A. order has been made, K. and husband cannot apply without consent of a person with PR.
Court would have to apply the welfare principle to arrive at a conclusion.

7(a). Sole ground for divorce is that the marriage has irretrievably broken down (M.C.A., s. 1(1)).
Ground can only be established by proof of one of five facts (M.C.A., s. 1(2)).

Can H. establish any one of the five facts now or in the future?

—he cannot petition on his own adultery (see s. 1(2)(a))
—he has "no complaint" about W., so cannot petition on her behaviour (s. 1(2)(b))

—he cannot petition on his own desertion in two year's time (see s. 1(2)(c))

—he needs consent of W. to petition under section 1(2)(d) in two year's time.

Only chance is for H. to wait until he and W. have been living apart for five years and petition under section 1(2)(e).

Will W. have a defence to a petition under section 1(2)(e)? W. could defend petition under the M.C.A., s. 5, *i.e.* on the ground that she would suffer grave financial or other hardship as a result of the decree. Defence applies only to petitions where sole fact alleged is under section 1(2)(e). Hardship must result from decree (*Talbot*). Loss of chance to benefit from H.'s pension—and chance is real, bearing in mind ages of parties—may be enough (*Julian*), unless H. can make up that loss. Will he have funds to do so in five years time? W.'s religious views probably not enough.

7(b). Sole ground for divorce would be that marriage has irretrievably broken down. Ground would only be proved by either H. or W. having filed a statement alleging this and thereafter having waited a year.

Thus, H. would start divorce process immediately and would not have to give any "reason" for marriage breakdown.

The one year period must be used for consideration of arrangements that must be made consequent upon divorce, *e.g.* finances. Parties should agree these matters. If this not possible, court could make orders under the M.C.A., s. 23 and s. 24.

At end of 11 months, H. could apply for divorce order which would be granted one month later, save in limited number of situations. In particular, current section 5 defence would be available to W.

8. *Do local authorities have "inadequate legal powers"?* CA has strengthened L.A. position in number of ways:

—ground for care/supervision orders no longer drawn in terms of specific (and complex) situations: L.A. less likely to fail on a "technicality"

—ground for care/supervision orders covers children at risk of future harm alone

—new child assessment order available

—legal effect of all orders clarified

—with leave, L.A. can apply for specific issue order or prohibited steps order, either by separate application or within family proceedings (CA, s. 10).

CA has curtailed L.A. position in number of ways:
—emergency protection order more limited in duration
—has duty to allow contact between child and parents: court can resolve all contact disputes
—parental rights resolution abolished.

Can local authorities resort to ward of court procedure?—only with leave (CA, s. 100): leave will not be granted unless court satisfied

(a) result which L.A. wish to achieve can only be achieved by use of wardship jurisdiction
(b) child likely to suffer significant harm if not warded.

NOTE: wardship jurisdiction cannot be used to grant care/supervision orders, any order requiring L.A. to accommodate child, any order conferring on L.A. power to determine any question concerning exercise of parental responsibility (CA, s. 100): (a) therefore difficult to satisfy.

9. It is unlikely that any undergraduate on a Family Law course will be asked to calculate a maintenance assessment. Therefore, for sometime, you will be asked to write an essay on the C.S.A. Be warned—avoid the criticism of the Agency beloved of the tabloid press and concentrate your answer on the legal issues raised by the question.

The C.S.A. was largely driven by the Government's desire to reduce public expenditure. Note "Children Come First" and the arguments for the establishment of the Agency.

Highlight in your answer:

—The "reduced benefit direction". Mothers must co-operate with the Agency at the risk of financial penalties.
—No allowance is made for previous "clean break agreements" which would have provided the child with a roof over his/her head.
—Mothers on state benefit suffer a pound for pound reduction.

—The "welfare of the child" is not first or paramount; only to be taken into account.

—The 1992 Regulations which reduce assessment where there is 104 nights contact, but exaggerate conflict between parents.

—Almost total exclusion of the Court's discretion.

INDEX